Praise for
The Naked Soul

"We are told that it is not good for human beings to be alone. Tim Gardner understands aloneness and has provided wisdom and light that point to a better way."

— JOHN ORTBERG, author of *Everybody's Normal Till You Get to Know Them* and *If You Want to Walk on Water, You've Got to Get Out of the Boat*

"*The Naked Soul* not only provides insight and help for your own struggles with loneliness, but it also does the same for that very lonely person right next door."

— DAVID AND CLAUDIA ARP, coauthors of *Loving Your Relatives* and the 10 Great Dates series

"Want authentic relationships? Want to stop letting technology rule you? Want to put loneliness behind you? Tim Gardner shows how to get real with God and find authentic love flowing from that relationship into the lives of people we know."

— EVERETT L. WORTHINGTON JR., author of *Forgiving and Reconciling*

"*The Naked Soul* unpacks why life is, for many of us, so lonely and mediocre. It offers hope through the difficult but fulfilling path to authentic life and relationship."

— DAVE RODRIGUEZ, senior pastor, Grace Community Church, Indianapolis, Indiana

"Whether you are young or approaching eighty, *The Naked Soul* is an essential read! Tim Gardner boldly and truthfully removes the guilt and frustration from loneliness and replaces them with understanding and authenticity. In the secret sectors of our hearts, we've had it wrong for so long! I'm now impassioned to bust out of my invisible cages and help others to do the same."

— HEATHER FLIES, junior high pastor, Wooddale Church,
    Minnesota & Youth Specialties CORE presenter

"Tim Gardner leads readers on a thought-provoking journey into the heart of human relationships. This book is a valuable resource for anyone hungering for authentic community."

— MARGARET FEINBERG, speaker and author of *Twentysomething:*
    Surviving & Thriving in the Real World and *God Whispers:*
    Learning to Hear His Voice

the
naked
soul

Tim Alan Gardner

the
naked
soul

God's amazing,

everyday solution

to loneliness

WATERBROOK
PRESS

THE NAKED SOUL
PUBLISHED BY WATERBROOK PRESS
2375 Telstar Drive, Suite 160
Colorado Springs, Colorado 80920
A division of Random House, Inc.

All Scripture quotations, unless otherwise indicated, are taken from the *Holy Bible, New International Version®*. NIV®. Copyright © 1973, 1978, 1984 by International Bible Society. Used by permission of Zondervan Publishing House. All rights reserved. Scripture quotations marked (AMP) are taken from *The Amplified Bible*. Old Testament, copyright © 1965, 1987 by The Zondervan Corporation. The Amplified New Testament, copyright © 1954, 1958, 1987 by The Lockman Foundation. Used by permission. Scripture quotations marked (MSG) are taken from *The Message*. Copyright © 1993, 1994, 1995, 1996, 2000, 2001, 2002. Used by permission of NavPress Publishing Group. Scripture quotations marked (NASB) are taken from the *New American Standard Bible®*. © Copyright The Lockman Foundation 1960, 1962, 1963, 1968, 1971, 1972, 1973, 1975, 1977, 1995. Used by permission. (www.Lockman.org). Some italics in Scripture quotations reflect the author's added emphasis.

Details in some anecdotes and stories have been changed to protect the identities of the persons involved.

ISBN 1-57856-839-0

Library of Congress Cataloging-in-Publication Data
Gardner, Tim Alan.
    The naked soul : God's amazing, everyday solution to loneliness / Tim Alan Gardner.— 1st ed.
       p. cm.
    Includes bibliographical references.
    ISBN 1-57856-839-0
    1. Loneliness—Religious aspects—Christianity. I. Title.
    BV4911.G37 2004
    248.8'6—dc22
                                    2004010765

Printed in the United States of America
2004—First Edition

10 9 8 7 6 5 4 3 2 1

To Austin, Caleb, and Grace

Being your dad has taught me more about how
our heavenly Father must feel toward His children
than any book, class, or person ever could.
Thank you for the vital and unique part
that each of you plays in a very "real" family,
full of laughter, fights, hugs, arguments,
games, drama, more laughter, fun, and love.
I wouldn't trade one moment.
Thank you for teaching me about authentic love.
May you always know you are loved.
May you know you never need to be lonely.
And may you be willing to risk
so that others may know love and relationship too.
I am beyond blessed.

Contents

Contents

Foreword

For five months Admiral Richard Byrd survived "one layer of darkness piled on top of the other."[1] He lived in a feeble shelter on the Ross Ice Barrier near the South Pole, enduring what has been described as the coldest place on the planet. The terrain was a sheet of ice thousands of feet thick with mountains of powdery snow shifting across its threatening surface. The temperature often dropped to eighty degrees below zero. In mid-April the sun dipped below the horizon and didn't return for weeks. The honored explorer suffered frostbite, carbon monoxide poisoning, disturbed sleep, and malnutrition.

When Admiral Byrd returned to civilization and wrote an account of his exploration, the title of his book did not emphasize the terrain, the weather, or the danger. A single word underscored the horror of being isolated from other people—*Alone*.

You don't have to suffer arctic cold to feel alone. Loneliness is experienced in bustling communities. More activity simply drives it deeper; crowds only make it worse.

The anguish of loneliness is defined better by experience than by a dictionary. It is being the last fifth grader chosen in a game of pickup baseball. It is denying yourself in order to serve your family's needs but never hearing a word of affirmation. It is trying something new and longing to share the experience with *anybody*. It is wondering why none of your friends really understands you and accepts you for who you are.

The book you are holding reveals the most helpful solution to loneliness I have ever encountered. If you fear Tim Gardner's advice will be trite or hackneyed, relax. You are about to encounter simple yet profound wisdom that is grounded in biblical understanding.

A half century ago David Riesman wrote a groundbreaking book, *The Lonely Crowd*, to describe how isolated many people feel even though they are constantly surrounded by others. Since then, magazines and best-selling books have suggested innumerable remedies: join a club, become more assertive, learn how to win friends, get married, get remarried, change jobs, travel, take up a hobby, volunteer. The perception is that getting busier will solve the problem. But this advice misses the heart of loneliness. We are not lonely because we lack activity and distractions.

Dr. Tim Alan Gardner understands the heart of loneliness like few people I know. Get ready to take an amazing journey through the pages of this book as you discover a new life of deep contentment and contagious joy. You are about to encounter the truth that God is yearning for you to experience: you are not alone.

Dr. Les Parrott, author of *Relationships*
Seattle Pacific University
Seattle, Washington

Acknowledgments

Writers are fond of stating that their books are always collaborative efforts and that without a huge group of people the book project would never get done. Well, that's true. But for me there is always just one person without whose complete support, tasks like this would never begin or end. That, of course, is my wonderful, beautiful, warm, encouraging prayer-supporter and best friend and favorite beachcomber partner—my wife, Amy. Thank you for authentically loving me for more than sixteen years. Your crowns in heaven will be many. I love you. May there forever be new beaches to explore.

Thank you again to my children—Austin, Caleb, and Grace—who don't always know "what daddy is working on in his office" and who usually can't go more than fifteen minutes without coming in and asking a question and who seem to forget that, when they crank up the electric guitar, drum set, and microphones upstairs, I can actually *hear* it in my office—directly below them. You have all touched my life in more ways than you'll ever know. You make me laugh. You each bring so much joy to my life. Thank you for all your support and love.

To my dad, Tim Gardner, for teaching me about commitment and hard work.

To my mom, Barbara Gardner, for giving me a love for books and words.

To Bill and Jane Schock, my in-laws, for making sure that store managers know they should carry my books, for keeping the kids at "Camp Grandma's," and for your love and support.

To Ron Lee, my editor extraordinaire; the work is always better because of you.

To Tara Strunk and Stacy Kahler, my cousin and her best friend. Thank you for sharing your hearts, insights, and experiences in the world of the twenty-somethings. Your thoughts will help many.

To all who have allowed me to enter their lives through retreats, classes, counseling relationships, and correspondence; you have taught me so much.

To all the folks at WaterBrook Press, for all the time you put into getting my ideas into everything from cool-looking book covers to marketing plans to print and to the store. Thank you, thank you.

To those who bought and continue to buy my first book, *Sacred Sex: A Spiritual Celebration of Oneness in Marriage,* so that WaterBrook actually wanted to do another book with me. Thank you to all who took time to send me notes and e-mails.

To the friends who have always supported my wacky ideas long before I was ever in print: Buddy, Debbie, Nick, LuAnn, Kurt, Vickie, Bud, Kristi, Mike, Jane, Dale, Lynn, Bill, Lisa, Mark and Judy (my brother and his wife), and Kent and Gabe (my other brother and his wife).

To all the writers and teachers who have taught me so much.

To Amy again—I just can't thank you enough.

And to God, the One who is the Word. The One who is the only perfect expression of authentic love and intimacy. The One who has blessed me beyond measure. And the One who sent His only Son, Jesus, into the world as the greatest gift of grace the world has ever known. Any truths in this book are His; any mistakes are mine. May this book be used to bring people closer to Him.

Find a Life That Matters

Nothing matters more to us than that we matter to someone. And we all long to have someone who matters to us.

But it doesn't stop there. We all want to live a life that matters to ourselves, and we want a life that matters to God. Yet instead we find ourselves frustrated, tired, impatient, hurried, angry, and passionless. Even more, we find ourselves lonely. Too often, our lives don't seem to matter much at all.

Isn't it weird that the deepest longings of our souls—the desire to know and be known and the yearning to love and be loved—remain largely unfulfilled? And this is true in spite of the fact that we have access to the most technologically advanced communication networks of all time. More than half of the American population is connected in a virtual online world (including more than 75 percent of teenagers), and 98 percent of Americans have at least one television (a higher percentage than have indoor plumbing!).[1] Doesn't it seem bizarre that while we're fully connected with the world we're also more alone? And this is neither a temporary nor an isolated phenomenon. Tragically, more and more young people are taking their own lives.

Does it make sense that everywhere you look, people are receiving pages or talking on cell phones, and yet the number of people being treated for depression (a condition often associated with emotional isolation) grew by more than five million reported cases over a recent decade?[2] We have Internet chat rooms, instant messaging, satellite television, computer dating, supermalls, megachurches, and three-way calling—and yet we are the loneliest and most disconnected society in a very, very long time.

Which of course begs the question: Why?

STILL LOOKING FOR LOVE

God designed us to seek the satisfaction that comes with naked-soul relationships. We're eager to trade empty relationships for the real thing. Yet where do we find that kind of love—honest, vulnerable, naked-and-without-shame love?

Since we're not very good at finding this type of love on our own, God shows us exactly how to get there. But let me warn you: the path that leads away from loneliness can be confusing, uncomfortable, even painful. It's a necessary path but not a safe one. It requires both trust and risk.

Leaving our loneliness behind forces us to let go of some familiar routines and comfortable habits. God never promised that fulfilling our longing for real love would be easy. He simply promised that He would always open a way for us. The path is there, and God invites us to begin the journey. It's up to each of us to decide if we're ready to release the pain of loneliness.

If you're not sure, think about last week—or the week before. If you've ever finished an eight-, ten-, or twelve-hour workday and at the end asked, "Is this all there is?" at least take a close look at what God has in store for you. If you're seldom alone but still certain that something big is missing from your life, then stop to find what it is. If you're in contact with more people than ever before but intimately known by no one, then ask yourself why.

It's possible to leave your aloneness behind. Just as God gave Adam the astounding gift of companionship that ended his stint of emotional isolation, you also can escape the death-dealing condition called loneliness. God invites you to trade the slow death of isolation for a full life packed with meaning and purpose and authentic love.

But know, too, that this journey is not just about you. In fact, it is primarily *not* about you. God does not put you in relationships just so you can have your own needs met. He wants you to enrich the lives of others—to change the world by being in naked-soul relationships. You are the solution to their loneliness just as they are called to chase loneliness from your life.

In the second chapter of Genesis, Adam and Eve experienced the absolute joy of not being alone. They were, as the Bible says, "naked and were not ashamed" (Genesis 2:25, NASB). They had nothing to hide, and they didn't even know it. They enjoyed the freedom of knowing and being known completely, of loving and being loved with abandon. But then, after they chose to disobey God, they adopted the soul-killing pattern of isolation. God came to them, as He undoubtedly had done many times before. But this time, instead of running to their Father with the joy of two-year-olds, they hid (see Genesis 3:8).

And we've been hiding ever since—from God and from one another.

But we don't have to hide. We can once again walk with God—and with others—in bold authenticity. We can fulfill our God-given purpose on earth. We can know the joy of naked-soul relationships.

The musical *Funny Girl* had it wrong. "People who need people" are not the luckiest people in the world.[3] People who need people are the *only* people in the world. There are no other kinds. There are simply those who do not know they need others.

Do you?

The chapters that follow show what God-honoring relationships look like—and what they don't—and how we can have the first and avoid the latter. The solutions are not designed for everyone else. They are crafted specifically for *you*.

It's time to come out of hiding.

It's time to leave your loneliness behind.

It's time to live a life that matters.

One

God Created Loneliness, Then He Solved It

So Don't Deny Your Deepest Need

> Loneliness is the leprosy of the modern world.
> —MOTHER TERESA

> If I'm such a legend, then why am I so lonely?
> —JUDY GARLAND

Do you want people to like you? I mean it. Do you want other people—even strangers—to like you?

I do. If I'm standing in line at the supermarket, surrounded by people I've never seen before, I want to appear likable. There's nothing in it for me, but for some reason I want everyone else to like me.

The need to be liked is a more powerful motivator than we realize. It affects how we present ourselves, how we view ourselves, and what choices we make. It can lead us to do or say things we otherwise would never do or say. But we don't talk much about our consuming desire to be liked. We just think about it a lot.

We like to think that being liked is a pretty simple process. I like you; you like me; we can all just be friends and get along.

If only it were that easy.

Think back on your life. I'd bet money that the desire to be liked by another person has been one of the most consuming, most enjoyable, most terrifying, most inspiring, and most devastating pursuits of your life. The way others choose to respond to us brings joy and fulfillment and also pain. That's the hard irony of relationships.

Remember those years of choosing sides for kickball, passing notes in class, getting parts in school plays, going to proms, being invited to parties— or *not* getting invited to a party and *not* being chosen for a team? The memories are still vivid. Every generation has its hit parade of songs that tell the sad story of loneliness. Roy Orbison, in a voice that cut to the quick, sang "only the lonely know how I feel."[1] The Beatles recognized "all the lonely people" and wondered "where do they all come from?"[2] In our own day, the indie rock group Bowling for Soup sings, "My loneliness is killing me."[3] And most baby boomers remember when Janis Ian's song "At Seventeen," about the loneliness of not fitting in, climbed to number three on the pop charts and received a Grammy nomination. And songs don't get more direct than the Janis Joplin lyric that states simply, "All is loneliness before me, loneliness before me."[4]

Every generation seeks a way to fit in, and every generation prays that no one will notice when they don't. It's important to have friends who love you. It's unbearably painful to be alone.

I recently attended a concert where I was twenty years older than 98 percent of the audience—and the audience was not made up of preschoolers. Relient K was on stage, a band popular among college-age Christians and my two boys. As is the custom at a concert such as this, most of the audience stood and crowded the stage, clapping, jumping, and sometimes running into one another while the band performed. It's all a part of being actively engaged in the music.

But I'm a midforties dude, and one of my sons was in a full-leg cast. My other son is shorter than the college-age fans, and as we made our way to our front-row seats we were enveloped by the crowd. We not only had to struggle to get to our seats (and then get people out of them), it was a struggle just to see the band.

I found myself playing an interesting mental game. The father side of me wanted to protect my boys and get them the great view from the front row that they'd been so excited about. The psychotherapist side of me was fascinated by this young crowd attempting to feel connected, to feel part of something and not be alone. Is standing so close that you can hardly move or breathe a cure for loneliness? Does being jammed together in a crowd make people feel they are liked and accepted? I know they wanted it to.

The Lessons of Not Being Liked

Our intense desire to be liked teaches us a great deal. Think back to the first time a parent or teacher told you: "If you want other children to like you, you have to play nicely with them." What did they mean "if"? Were they kidding? Using the word *if* implies that maybe, just maybe, we may *not* want people to like us. It also plants the idea in our heads that there just might be people who in fact *don't* like us, so we'll have to work really hard to turn that around. Or even worse, we begin to fear that just being who we are will make people not like us.

We learn that being unliked and unlikable is a very real possibility.

Then we grow up, or at least our bodies do. And we learn that there are people out there who in fact do not like us. We find that there are things about the way we look, the way we talk, where we grew up, or simply who we are that cause others not to want to be around us. And we learn that there are things we don't even like about ourselves. We wish we looked different, acted differently, hadn't made all the mistakes we've made. We're adults, but we're all still standing out there on the playground, waiting to be picked for the team, hoping someone will like us just the way we are.

In the movie *The Truth About Cats and Dogs,* a friend of veterinarian Abby Barnes comments: "Disappointment [from a dating relationship] doesn't kill."

"You're right," Abby responds, "disappointment doesn't kill. Rejection kills. Disappointment only maims."[5]

We already know the force of this in the core of our being. It was God who said, "It is not good for the man to be alone" (Genesis 2:18).

I vividly remember the day one of my childhood buddies came for a visit. His name was Tim, like mine, and he had moved out of our neighborhood. Now he was back to play for a day, and I was one excited eight-year-old. Tim and I were playing in my yard when Jimmy, the third member of the Tim-Tim-Jim trio, rode his bike into my driveway. This was cool; we were all together again!

Jimmy hung out for a few minutes in my yard, then he said something about wanting Tim to go look at his bike. The two of them walked off, and as I waited for them to return I saw Jimmy peddling down the hill toward his house—with Tim riding double on his bike. All I could do was look down at my feet and feel very alone and very rejected.

That was more than thirty years ago. You could tell me I should just get over it, but it wouldn't do any good. I can see it happening in front of me right now. I'm a licensed mental health counselor, for goodness sake, and here I am writing about something that happened when I was eight. *You* are certainly not stuck on something that insignificant from your childhood. Or maybe you are.

We all are marked by rejection. If you think you're not, then scan your memory for an image like Jimmy and Tim riding off to have fun without you. Your picture will be different, but the impact is largely the same. Being rejected by those we care about is one of the most devastating experiences along the human journey. Having someone choose to play with someone other than you hurts. Not being liked maims us.

Recently a team of mental health counselors and medical doctors conducted an experiment to try to determine reasons for the sharp rise in emotional and behavioral problems among youth. For the most part, the teenagers studied were well educated, techno-savvy, and from financially secure families. Yet 25 percent of them were at risk of failing to function productively in adulthood. Why? The researchers concluded that "humans are 'hardwired' biologically to need close connections with others." Further, "religion and spirituality" are vital in a person's life. Therefore, "when both belonging and belief are absent, children are more likely to experience physical, emotional, and spiritual crisis."[6] Being lonely is deadly.

THE LESSONS OF BEING LIKED

Now consider the opposite power of actually being *liked* by someone. I can vividly recall the image of my lovely wife, Amy, the first time I felt she might like me. We were working at a Young Life camp in the Rocky Mountains. It was Tableau Night, and we were decked out in 1800s garb. I was the sheriff, she was the schoolmarm. Seventy-some-odd camp staffers were waiting for some four hundred high school campers to descend the stairs and be surprised that they had suddenly "traveled back in time."

I stood in the back of a wagon, looking for the signal that the teenagers were coming. Amy stood forty feet away in front of a group of unruly "students." Our eyes met; she smiled. No, it wasn't the first time a woman had ever smiled at me, as some who know me may think. And it wasn't the first time I had seen Amy smile. But this smile wasn't a smile of, well, just smiling. It was a smile that meant more, as though she had enjoyed the few times we had spent talking and liked seeing me now. *That* was cool.

I can see that smile today. Why? Well, it helps that I have been married to her for more than sixteen years, so I've seen that smile many times (as well as "the look" that means something entirely different, but we won't get into that now). But I remember *that* smile on *that* day.

The memory is vivid because the yearning to connect and be loved is the fiercest longing of the human soul. I remember that smile because being liked brings life to my soul.

Every time we try to connect and it fails, a scar is left on our heart. In contrast, each time we reach out to love someone and are loved in return, our heart smiles.

That's why we all want to be liked.

Why God Put Us Here

But wait. Surely we weren't put on earth to wear ourselves out trying to get other people to like us. There has to be more.

Most of us also have a driving desire to make a real difference in this world—be it an invention, a medical breakthrough, leading others in a crisis situation, or saving a life (or a soul). Or on a smaller scale, to mentor someone, to reflect God's love into the lives of those who need to know Him, to be a friend to those in need of support. In big ways and small, we want our lives to count.

It's good that we want to change the world, but we might not understand what it actually takes. The simple truth is that by investing in relationships, we really can make a difference. An eternal difference. In fact, it's what God has called us to do. One by one, person to person, we are to "go and make disciples of all nations" (Matthew 28:19). In other words, we are called to invest in people and change the world.

Pursuing the types of relationships that bring about real change is rewarding but not always pleasant. Consider the way Jesus prepared His followers for the mission of changing the world:

> All men will hate you because of me, but he who stands firm to
> the end will be saved. (Mark 13:13)

> Blessed are you when men hate you,
> when they exclude you and insult you
> and reject your name as evil,
> because of the Son of Man. (Luke 6:22)

These aren't verses you see printed on fliers designed to get people to visit a church. Churches instead promise that we'll find friendly people who will like us. So how do we reconcile the apparent contradiction? We long to be liked and to connect with others. Yet there is Jesus's warning about being hated just for following Him.

Are we here to love others and to be loved in return? Or are we here to change the world and risk opposition and hatred? The answer is yes to both.

God created us with a desire to be intimately connected to others and to feel the emptiness of life when we're rejected. The first thing declared to be "not good" in the creation of the world was that Adam was alone. Our head tells us loneliness is bad. Our heart tells us loneliness is bad. God tells us loneliness is bad. There is no question: it's bad to be alone.

God created Adam as a person who needed to be connected to others in relationships. There was nothing sinful about his feeling lonely. God created the need. But clearly, it's not good, so He didn't leave him that way.

What is good is to be connected to others in naked-soul relationships. So just as God created the need, He also delivered the solution. God's answer to Adam's loneliness was to create another person, Eve. He created Adam as a being who craved and needed the companionship of others. And then God chose people—not Himself—to meet this God-given need.

Most believers won't question the assertions that we need God and that we need Christ in order to have a relationship with God. But there seems to be a great deal of hesitancy when it comes to admitting that we also need people. At least we often fail to admit it by the way we live, keeping our true selves hidden behind the walls of our houses and the walls of our faces. And after all, isn't God enough?

God answers that question with one word: no. When it comes to relationships, we need more than God alone. We need one another. But instead of admitting our need for authentic intimacy, we insist on hiding behind a mask, because we believe the lie that masks protect us from hurt, from being misunderstood, from walking into an emotional buzz saw. A mask pretends to serve as a protective shield, promising to deflect criticism, unjust accusations, and emotional turmoil.

The mask lies.

Instead of protecting us, masks destroy us with a false sense of safety and security. The masks serve only to prolong our isolation and to amplify our loneliness. Masks prevent people from caring about us and caring for us, because they make it impossible for anyone to really know us. God tells us that we need people, while masks lie and tell us that we're fine just hanging out with God.

Getting tight with God is not enough. We need to be tight with God *and* in intimate, honest, vulnerable relationships with other people. That is God's solution to our need to be liked, and, interestingly, it's also the path we follow in changing the world. In meeting our own needs to be loved, we find ourselves loving others and changing the world.

That's why we're here.

WHY WE'RE SO BAD AT THIS

Why do we fail so miserably at fulfilling our God-given purpose? It's not as though we're bad at needing people, because we all do—whether we acknowledge it or not. What we often seem to fall short on is letting ourselves experience the fulfillment of that need through authentic God-honoring relationships.

But why cheat ourselves out of the very thing we want the most? I can think of several reasons.

First, too many of us don't recognize the importance of knowing and loving others in God's grand economy of life. So instead, we try to fill our need for authentic relationships with a thousand other things, ranging from sex to status to substances.

Second, knowing how to be a good "knower and lover" is not part of the human DNA, at least not since the fruit-eating rebellion that was launched in the Garden of Eden. We like to think we are naturally great lovers, husbands, wives, and friends. It's not true. We need to let God train us in knowing and loving others.

13

Third, we are scared. Really knowing someone else is risky, and being known by others can be downright frightening. And love? Man, that's skydiving without a parachute.

Fourth, we're bad at knowing and being known, loving and being loved, for the same reason we have problems with any relationship—one of us is selfish. Okay, we're *all* selfish. And selfishness is both the cause and the result of the fact that we are sinners.

Yeah, we're sinners. It's fifth on this list, but it ranks first among our problems. Being selfish and being a sinner gives us one top priority in every relationship: me. Or in your case: you. "What can you do for me? Why aren't you doing more for me? Don't you know that you need to be paying attention to me and taking care of me and thinking about me?"

The great truth of relationships is that the more we worry about ourselves, the less we'll have a chance to experience true intimacy with another person. Authentic intimacy comes by learning to risk. God's plan for intimacy is risky because it involves focusing on someone else, a person other than ourselves, and that's not our natural tendency.

Late-night-television host Conan O'Brien described hosting the television Emmy awards this way: "You're standing in front of the most self-involved audience you're ever going to stand in front of. It's like a narcissists convention."[7] That may be true of the typical Hollywood crowd. And yet it seems that if he were standing in front of many church congregations on Sunday morning, O'Brien could say the same thing. We all carry membership cards to the National Narcissists Society.

What Now?

As we have seen, Jesus told us we would be hated for being His followers, so why worry about the fact that we are not very good at letting ourselves need others and be needed by others? In the midst of all of the other crises in the world, why should we even care how good or bad we are at dealing with interpersonal relationships?

For one, because we're cheating ourselves. By not being involved in thoroughly authentic relationships, we are missing out on a huge blessing that God wants us to enjoy. Letting ourselves be known and loved not only fulfills the yearnings of our soul, but it also is where we experience the community that can provide a place to heal our hurts and end our loneliness. And it's the place where we can contribute to the healing of others.

The second answer is that living in an environment of genuine love and acceptance with others is one of the primary ways Christ taught us to bring His message of God's grace. In other words, learning to live in authentic relationships *is how we change the world.* Likewise, refusing to live in authentic relationships is how we let the world continue to spiral away from its Creator. So if you're not ready to make this change for your own benefit, then do it so you can reflect the love of God into the lives of others.

The key both to ending our loneliness and to taking the first step to changing the world is as close as the people next door. Maybe even as close as the people who live in your home. It is imperative that we learn to love and be loved. But to get started, we must choose to love.

> I've loved you the way my Father has loved me. Make yourselves
> at home in my love. If you keep my commands, you'll remain
> intimately at home in my love....
>
> I've told you these things for a purpose: that my joy might be
> your joy, and your joy wholly mature. This is my command:
> *Love one another the way I loved you.* This is the very best way to
> love. Put your life on the line for your friends. You are my friends
> when you do the things I command you. (John 15:9–14, MSG)

Being liked can't be our goal. For that matter, neither can changing the world or living a life that matters. Those are results. Our goal is to be obedient to Christ.

But by being obedient to Christ, we will change the world, and we will have an abundance of life-enhancing relationships along the way. We will love and be loved in a way that makes a lonely world stand up and take notice. And we'll get rid of our own loneliness.

Do you want to be loved? Do you want to change the world? Congratulations. You can begin right now.

Reflection

The Big Idea
God created love. He also created loneliness. Then God created the amazing, everyday answer to loneliness—He gave Adam and Eve what the Bible describes as the naked-and-unashamed relationships that abolish aloneness. He shows us how to love and be loved and how to experience the life-giving power of the naked-soul experience. God designed each of us to be in authentic, life-changing relationships with other people. It is our call to decide what we will do in response to God's solution to loneliness.

Key Verse
"GOD said, 'It's not good for the Man to be alone; I'll make him a helper, a companion.'" (Genesis 2:18, MSG)

Answering Questions
- Are you willing to let God challenge your view of relationships, even if it involves significant risk?

- Are you willing to honestly look at the things in your life that may be keeping you from impacting your corner of the world for God?
- Are you ready to let go of loneliness and live a life that matters?

Prayer

Loving Father, thank You that You have made me just as You desired. And thank You for putting people in my life to end my loneliness and so I can put an end to their loneliness. Help me as I begin this journey to discover what it means to live a life that changes the world. Father, send Your Spirit to guide and bless this journey. Amen.

Two

Alone or Just Lonely?

How the Wrong Friendships Fuel Our Loneliness

The seriousness and importance of friendship is masked
for some people by a characteristic which is really its glory:
it is unnecessary. It is arbitrary, a thing of choice.

—C. S. Lewis

Do you have any friends?

Most people would quickly answer, "Well, of course." So maybe a better question would be, "What type of friends and friendships do you have?" We don't just need friends; we need the right type of friends.

Here are some inarguable truths about friends:

- Not having any can destroy you.
- Not thinking you need any can destroy you.
- Having the wrong kind can destroy you.
- Thinking that you have to be with friends all the time, that you can't live without them, or that your friends are the most important thing in your life can destroy you.

If friends are essential to our well-being, then how can friendship be so dangerous? Let's look first at how these four truths about friendship reveal themselves; then we'll look at the practical impact that friends and friendships have on our daily lives.

No Friends?

Not having friends can kill you, or at least cut your life short. "Loneliness, while largely overlooked, ranks as one of the most lethal risk factors determining who will live and who will die prematurely in modern industrialized nations," writes Dr. James Lynch in *A Cry Unheard*.[1] Being lonely—defined as not having any significant relationships—is a reliable predictor that a person will meet with an early death. It's another type of silent killer.

Other studies have shown that unmarried adults have mortality rates that are 50 percent higher for women and a whopping 250 percent higher for men, compared with married adults. For men, being single is more deadly than heart disease. Researchers have shown that "having heart disease shortens the average man's life span by slightly less than six years. But being unmarried chops almost ten years off a man's life. Similarly, not being married will shorten a woman's life span by more years than would being married and having cancer or living in poverty."[2]

God came up with the solution to our loneliness in part to relieve sadness and isolation. But even more, God knew that it's "not good" for a person to be alone because it's deadly. We have heard of people dying for a drink, dying for a cigarette, even dying for a cause. But all around us people are dying to know and be known, to love and be loved. People are dying for a friend. And it may even be you.

Don't Need Friends?

In the fourth century BC, Aristotle correctly said, "A man wholly solitary would be either a god or a brute." Today it would seem that we have many people—especially men—who must believe they are brutes. Or perhaps they are turning into brutes. While most of us long for more friends or for a really close friend, there are those who *choose* to forgo close friendships. And making the choice to be friendless, versus trying but failing to find friends, does not negate the dangerous effects of loneliness.

Being alone—no matter the cause—has been linked to an increased rate of certain types of cancer, a reduced level of educational and work-related accomplishments, elevated blood pressure, higher stress and diminished levels of mental health, and greater difficulty in recovering from trauma.[3] Research has demonstrated the amazingly beneficial effects of human contact and closeness to those who are ill, injured, or dying—and the overwhelmingly negative consequences to a person in those same circumstances who has no physical and emotional connections with others.

Dr. Lynch tells of watching a man as he lay for fourteen days motionless and comatose in a hospital bed. The man had been severely injured, and the injury, combined with drugs he had been given, left him paralyzed, able to breathe only with the help of a machine. Even more heartbreaking was the fact that during the two weeks between the injury and the man's death, not one person ever visited him.

On the afternoon of the fourteenth day, a decision was made to remove the life-support equipment. Shortly after the life-giving machines were shut down, a kind nurse came in to comfort this paralyzed, comatose, lonely man. All she did—which turned out to be a tremendous amount—was simply hold and stroke the man's hand. Lynch, an expert in stress and cardiovascular rehabilitation, writes that he "watched with a sense of semi-paralyzed amazement as this man's heart rate and heart rhythm changed just as soon as" the nurse began to touch him.[4]

Remember I said physical *and* emotional connection? What did human touch mean to the unconscious dying man? Was it simply a neurological response to a physical stimulus? No, I don't think so. What happened was that this failing life finally felt the warmth of another human being who cared. Finally, a lonely man no longer felt lonely. And a nurse was doing her part in changing the world. When the man died, he didn't feel as isolated. His heart showed it.

THE WRONG FRIENDS?

Regardless of your religious upbringing, you most likely heard this proverb when you were growing up: "Bad company corrupts good morals." This wisdom is found in the Bible, in 1 Corinthians 15:33 (NASB). If you didn't hear it from your parents, you certainly heard it from a teacher or scout leader or other concerned adult. And there's more to this proverb than simply the corruption of morals. When bad company leads to corrupt actions and the whole gang gets caught, you often stand and suffer on your own—with no support from the rest of the bad company.

I remember my first junior high detention-hall experience. Actually, I remember the moment I got caught "doing the deed" that earned me the detention. I was in history class, which was where I was supposed to be. But I happened to be standing on top of my desk, arm drawn all the way back, a fraction of a second away from drilling the guy a few seats behind me with a baseball-sized spit wad. That's when the door opened and in walked someone other than my teacher. (I was hoping for the teacher, because she liked me.) Instead, it was the vice principal. She glared and gave me the universal gesture for "Get down off that desk, and get your tail out in the hallway this instant!"

After the eternal walk to the gallows, I had to endure the inevitable question: "Tim, why were you acting like that?" The standard response is, "Well, you see, the other kids were doing it too. And, yes, I just *might* jump off a cliff if everyone else did." (Okay, I didn't say that last part…but I thought it.)

The spit-wad incident was minor, but there are more examples than we can list of friends having a deadly impact on others. In the last few years we've read the horror of the Columbine High School massacre, the DC-area sniper murders, any number of violent high school and college hazing incidents. Then there are instances that hit closer to home. A formerly faithful spouse is "talked into" having an affair. A teenager gets drunk and then gets behind the wheel of a car because someone says it's the cool thing to do. A man goes with friends to a "gentlemen's club" because, you know, it's just "entertainment." People who would never do a harmful thing on their own end up jumping off a cliff because it seems that everyone else is doing it—and getting away with it. It's true that friends either give us moral support or immoral support.

Bad friends lead to bad things and then leave us to suffer alone, when being alone was the very thing we were seeking to avoid. Ironic, isn't it?

Do You Really *Have* to Be with Friends?

My wife and I recently spent an evening with a group of twenty-somethings discussing their lives and relationships. They talked openly about friends who frequently drink too much, engage in casual sex, and party too hard. They spoke of a near compulsion to "have to go out and be with friends." When I asked why, they gave two answers—one that reflects the surface of their lives and one that reveals the inner workings of their hearts.

"You don't want people to think you're a loser who has to stay home." That's the social reason, the motivation on the surface. But then they added, "Because we don't want to be alone." That's the heart reason.

To avoid being alone, they join in all sorts of activities they don't enjoy. When asked what they would *prefer* to do, my twenty-something friends mentioned a really simple thing: just to be at home—or somewhere else—with some *really good friends*. Friends who didn't expect them to behave a certain way or to participate in anything they would prefer to skip. But instead of enjoying this freedom in friendships, they surrendered to the inner pressure of "I have to go out."

There is momentary fun in superficial relationships but also the ache of long-term regret. There is the shame from yet another night of casual and unfulfilling sex, and there is the emptiness that is felt when all the party folks go home and we discover we're still intensely *lonely*.

Here's the point. (You might want to underline this part.) There's a huge difference between the desire to not be lonely and the feeling that you *have* to be with another person. We need to be connected with others in authentic relationships, but we don't have to fit in. The two are not the same.

As Dr. Hawkeye Pierce said in a moment of *M*A*S*H* wisdom, "Loneliness is everything it is cracked up to be." When given the choice between being by ourselves or doing something that will temporarily dampen our loneliness, we feel compelled to do the latter. And that's true even when we know we'll probably regret it the next morning.

THE SOLUTION TO A LAME WEEKEND

When we just can't stand being lonely any longer, we're experiencing a God-given emotion. But being with others is not the same thing as not being lonely. God designed us to be in relationship with others, but not just any relationship. His design calls for *authentic* relationships. If we believe that we have significance only if we have someone in our lives, then we'll try to stuff people (or alcohol or sex or parties or work or noise) into a void they can never fill. And that quest will leave us more alone—and more lonely. It's another irony. Spending more and more time with people can actually fuel our loneliness.

Think of situations where people talk about how cool it was over the weekend when they "got wasted." These days, wasting oneself or one's weekend or one's life is considered cool. How sincere can a friendship be when no one talks about what is really going on inside his head and heart? How fulfilling can it be to be surrounded by people—or even to spend time with just one person—when they do not truly know you? How can there be "love" when there is no "naked soul"?

Feeling pressured to have friends forces you into artificial relationships and always leads to frustration. You're searching for a friend who truly knows you and loves you no matter what. Those friends are never found in the compulsive, superficial relationships of pressured friendship.

Now that we're bummed out about friends and friendship, where does all of this leave us? Should we just turn off the phone and pretend we're not home?

Not yet. There is still hope, and it's because God designed answers just as He designed our problem of loneliness. The frustrations of superficial relationships should push us to turn to God to find out how He, the creator of our desires, intended for our loneliness to be solved.

God has given us certain needs that can only be met in Him. We need to identify those needs and seek God for their fulfillment. But we also need to understand other driving needs that God has not promised to meet in Himself. He tells us we'll find fulfillment for those needs only in real relationships with other people. Too often we confuse the two.

When the prophet Nathan confronted King David concerning his sexual affair with a married woman and the ensuing plot to have her husband killed, the first place David turned was to God. At the end of Nathan's rebuke, Scripture says the king's response was, "I have sinned against the LORD" (2 Samuel 12:13).

In Psalm 51, David sings his remorse:

> Have mercy on me, O God,
>   according to your unfailing love;
> according to your great compassion
>   blot out my transgressions.
> Wash away all my iniquity
>   and cleanse me from my sin.
>
> For I know my transgressions,
>   and my sin is always before me.
> Against you, you only, have I sinned
>   and done what is evil in your sight,
> so that you are proved right when you speak
>   and justified when you judge. (Psalm 51:1–4)

When we experience moral failure, the One we have ultimately failed is God. David knew that God was the only One who could cleanse him from his sin. He needed to make things right with people, but he *first* needed to make things right with God (see 1 John 1:9).

Our relationship with God gives us ultimate significance and purpose on earth. We are His children (John 1:12), we are His "workmanship," created in Jesus Christ to do good works for Him (Ephesians 2:10), and we have been given the phenomenal responsibility of taking the message of

His love and forgiveness to the world (Acts 1:8). It is our Father in heaven who ultimately gives our hearts the peace we so desperately desire (Philippians 4:7) and who gives us the assurance of His eternal sovereignty over our souls (Matthew 10:28). Significance, forgiveness, cleansing, and purpose are needs that are fulfilled only by God.

The answer to the question "Who am I?" is found in knowing God as our Creator and Savior. However, the answer to a second question, "Why am I here?" is found in experiencing authentic relationships with other people. God alone answers the first question, while naked-soul relationships with others answer the second question.

When God saw the problem of human loneliness, He chose to meet that need with other humans. It is God who created marriage (Mark 10:6–8) and who "sets the lonely in families" (Psalm 68:6). It is God who tells us to visit those who are sick and in prison (see Matthew 25:34–45) and to care for the "orphans and widows in their distress" (James 1:27). Human relationships are both life-giving and life-protecting, one of the ways that God overcomes the destruction of loneliness.

THE TENSION OF BEING CONNECTED

As we have noted, authentic relationships don't come naturally. For instance, it's not second nature to us that we receive the most when we give freely to others. It seems as if it should be the other way around. And here's the mother of all relational paradoxes: authentic relationships require both deep intimacy and clearly defined individuality. In other words, being intimately connected to another person works only if you are a whole, complete, and completely separate individual. Connected yet fully independent. That's the key.

Even those who may not have a personal relationship with their Creator have spoken of the need to strike a balance between intimacy and independence. A quick survey of the major personality theorists, including Sigmund Freud and Harry Stack Sullivan, shows them dabbling in what God has always told us to be true: we need a strong, clear individual identity, *and* we need significant amounts of interpersonal intimacy. The two together make us a person who is truly alive. As Christians, we know that to be fully awake to the world is to know and be known, to love and be loved, by the One who made us through Jesus Christ. But we must also know that God designed us to be fully invested in the lives of others—and to allow others to be fully invested in our lives. The journey God has put us on involves knowing and being known by others in a way that creates a three-way intimacy between ourselves, our God, and authentic friends.

In spite of his many shortcomings, Freud had a few things right. In an article on narcissism (defined as an infatuation and obsession with oneself to the exclusion of all others), Freud wrote that "the individual does actually carry on a twofold existence: one to serve his own purpose, and the other as a link in a chain [i.e., relationships]."[5] He goes on to explain that when we are young, it's natural to be more concerned with our own needs. But if we mature as adults, we will become equally concerned about the welfare of other people. Hence, intimacy and individuality.

Psychiatrist Harry Stack Sullivan, from the school of neosocialism, disagreed with Freud about the centrality of sexuality in mental disorders, but he agreed with him, in effect, when he suggested that people "must be viewed from the view of the person's striving for and concern with self-esteem and the esteem of others in an interpersonal context."[6] Sullivan believed that true individuality could only be developed within true intimacy. We define ourselves, in part, in and through our relationships. But we can never expect others to be our sole source of self-purpose.

We have to stand on our own as individuals, and we have to stand together with others in intimate, interconnected relationships. Without one of these two dimensions, we lack our full identity as persons.

Drs. Les and Leslie Parrott, a clinical psychologist and a family therapist, have identified a human tendency that they call the "compulsion for completion." In a quest for personal wholeness we begin to believe things like: "If I find the right person, my life will be complete. I need this person to be complete. [And] if this person needs me, I will be complete."[7] It's healthy to seek the solution to the empty space in our life. But it's unhealthy to believe that we are somehow "completed" by another human.

"If you try to find intimacy with another person before achieving a sense of identity on your own," the Parrotts explain, "all your relationships will become an attempt to complete yourself."[8] Completion in our lives and in our hearts is *not* found by having friends or even by getting married. Completion is found by knowing who God is and understanding who we are in God. We are complete in God, first and only. Then we are ready to end our aloneness through authentic relationships with others.

Jamie exemplified this struggle. A twenty-eight-year-old single mother, she had never in her life felt complete. At the age of fourteen, she learned the power of the female body. Boys liked to look at her and touch her. She knew they liked looking and touching, but she mistakenly thought they liked *her*.

The day she walked into my counseling office, I could see that she had mastered the power of female sexuality. She wore a short black skirt and a form-fitting top that dropped low enough to expose much of her breasts. Jamie's life story was cluttered with boyfriends and one short-term marriage. She acknowledged that she had sex with everyone she went out with more than once. She had even come to believe that if a guy *didn't* try to get her to bed by the second date, there was something wrong with him.

But Jamie wasn't a sex addict. She didn't even enjoy it all that much. She simply believed that sex equaled acceptance and love and being wanted by someone else. Sex made her feel complete because having a boyfriend made her feel complete.

But now, as she approached age thirty, she wondered why she still felt so desperately lonely. She thought she just needed to learn how to "feel more loved." What she really needed was to find that she was loved by God—completely and without limit. She had to find completion as a person on her own with God and without men. Only then could her loneliness be healed through authentic relationships with others who didn't care how she looked or what she would do for them.

While doing therapy with those who are struggling to find wholeness in the midst of a relationship, I often draw three sets of circles to help people understand this concept. (See page 31.)

I have drawn these sets of circles for married couples only to watch lights pop on in their heads. I've drawn the circles for teenagers who pull back, reluctant to take the risk of finding a real "us" in their relationship. I've spoken with young adults who feel they're too busy to figure out the individuality piece or just not convinced that they really need to take the chance on intimacy. And they are all lonely.

If we don't know who we are, or if we don't like who we are, we will spend our lives in the top two sets of circles. We will either keep ourselves separate from others and lose out on intimacy, or we will become completely enmeshed in another person, as Jamie had done repeatedly, and we'll lose our individuality. Both conditions indicate that we don't know our identity in Christ. In that state, we will never have real friends. We will never be a real friend to others. We will never offer hope to a lonely world.

By God's master blueprint, we find out *who* we are in Him. We find significance and security in life by doing the hard work of self-inspection that, when conducted in the recesses of our hearts, will lead us into a personal relationship with God. We find that we are complete in God and only in God.

At the same time, we find out *why* we're here as we pursue authentic relationships with other people. The end to our loneliness is found in vulnerable and intimate relationships with others. By doing the God part of this work first, we are able to move toward authenticity with others. That is what's represented by the third set of circles.

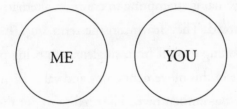

two independent people without intimacy

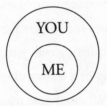

one person enmeshed with another, no individuality

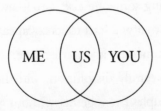

intimacy and individuality

THE DAILY DANCE

One of the saddest realities of life is when someone is married and yet is still lonely. The same can be said of those who show up at church on Sunday morning and find themselves surrounded by people seeking to learn about God, yet they are still lonely. It's the same story with teenagers who are lost to hours of instant messaging or twenty-somethings who rush from work to the gym to the clubs but still feel incredibly lonely.

There is a "new movement," as the news media have called it, among twenty-somethings that is attempting to create an alternative to the "I want to get married" crowd. They frown on the term *single* because it implies that a person is looking to shift from singleness to being part of a married couple. The people in this movement enjoy and value friendships, but they also are content to be on their own. They refuse to put their lives on hold while they wait for a mate to come along. They've got it!

Well, at least to a point. Part of the motivation behind this movement is the assumption that relationships are temporary. They feel that failed marriages are inevitable, so while they recognize their need for other people, they fully expect aloneness to be a recurring reality of life. Such a mind-set is self-fulfilling. If you fear the ending of a relationship, you will naturally protect yourself from expected hurt. Whether you realize it or not, you will hold back in your relationships. You may allow your life to overlap ever so slightly with another person's, but you'll never fully commit and you'll never fully abandon yourself to loving someone else. You'll always be looking for the crack in the relationship that will lead to its collapse.

I understand their concerns about marriage. They have experienced tremendous hurt due to family dissolution, and they want to avoid it in their own lives. Many couples live together without getting married because they are trying to find some assurance that a future marriage will actually work. They see cohabitation as a way to guard against the pain of a future divorce. They don't realize, however, that couples who live together prior to marriage actually experience divorce rates 50 percent higher than those who don't. Why? Because a strong, lasting relationship is not about being able to live with somebody for a while. And it's certainly not about being lucky enough to find the perfect partner. Strong relationships are made by choice—a daily choice to love—and by risk.

This movement is understandable. It is, however, not the answer. Seeking friendships while preparing for the expected end of those relationships will simply mask the loneliness at the core of our soul.

Jesus prayed to His Father:

> The same glory you gave me, I gave them,
> So they'll be as unified and together as we are—
> I in them and you in me.
> Then they'll be mature in this oneness,
> And give the godless world evidence
> That you've sent me and loved them
> In the same way you've loved me. (John 17:22–23, MSG)

Jesus prayed that *we* would learn the dance of intimacy and individuality just as He did in the relationship with His Father.

Another memory from my childhood (and this one didn't lead to detention hall) is of the day my late grandfather opened Arkie's Dessau Dance Hall in Dessau, Texas. In the early 1970s, this *really cool* place hosted the best local bands, drew huge crowds every weekend, and boasted the largest dance floor in all of central Texas. As a kid, I was enamored with all the glitz, glamour, and hoopla of a real-live Texas dance hall, and I completely missed the main reason that women and men from the likes of

Austin, Pflugerville, Turkey Hollow, Thrall, Hutto, Jollyville, and beyond flocked there three nights a week: they came to be together; they came to dance.

It really doesn't matter if you hate the kind of dancing that involves music and a dance partner; it really doesn't matter if you have two left feet or can't carry a tune in a bucket. It doesn't even matter if you think this analogy of dancing is really, really stupid. The truth of God's Word and God's world is that He created you and me to be in relationship with other people. Whether or not we realize it, He created us to dance. And being "in relationship" involves much more than simply knowing a person's name, profession, or golf handicap. Being in an authentic relationship with another person means putting yourself in a position to let God use you to eliminate the first and most important "not good" that exists in another person's life. That person is alone, which is something you can change. We dance because we want to connect with other people. Dancing means an end to loneliness.

DANCE WISELY

As C. S. Lewis said, "The seriousness and importance of friendship is masked for some people by a characteristic which is really its glory: it is unnecessary. It is arbitrary, a thing of choice."[9] Friends are a serious and important business. And having them is a choice. We choose not to have authentic friendships at our own peril. Remember, it's deadly. Literally. But it's also deadly to the world at large. We choose not to have true friends or to be a true friend at the risk of not changing a lonely world.

Having true friends is a God-given privilege and blessing. Jesus Himself gave us the great honor of being His friend. He told His disciples, "I'm no longer calling you servants because servants don't understand what their master is thinking and planning. No, I've named you friends because I've let you in on everything I've heard from the Father" (John 15:15, MSG). Christ shared with us the glory of His Father, the glory of heaven, the glory of salvation. That is the glory of His friendship with us. Friends know and share what truly matters in life.

We can't change the world without authentic relationships. We can't change our own world without being a friend and allowing friends into our lives. Ask yourself, "Who are my friends, and why do I need them?" Then answer a second question: "What type of friend am I to others?"

To be a friend and to allow others to be your friend, you first need to complete the hard work of becoming whole in God without expecting any other person to complete you. It is God who gives you your identity and meaning. It is God who gives you the strength to reach out to others in naked-soul relationships. In response to the commands of our greatest Friend, we live a life that matters, and we change the world.

In *The Message*, Eugene Peterson translates Paul's closing words to the Christians at Thessalonica like this:

> One final word, friends. We ask you—*urge* is more like it—that
> you keep on doing what we told you to do to please God, not in
> a dogged religious plod, but in a living, spirited dance. (1 Thessa-
> lonians 4:1, MSG)

We are called to be whole in Christ. Then we are called out of that wholeness to be friends with those who are lonely, those who are far from God, and those who are just sitting off to the side of the dance floor, hoping one day to be able to join the dance of intimacy and individuality.

God calls us to dance.

Reflection

The Big Idea

God created us to develop a healthy sense of individuality separate from others by finding our identity and meaning in Him. He also created us to enjoy relational intimacy with friends—the right kind of friends. By knowing who we are in God and by investing in authentic relationships with others, we demonstrate the love of God to the world.

Key Verse

"My prayer is not for them alone. I pray also for those who will believe in me through their message, that all of them may be one, Father, just as you are in me and I am in you. May they also be in us so that the world may believe that you have sent me." (John 17:20–21)

Answering Questions

- Spend some time thinking about your friendships. Are they based on honesty and authenticity? Compare your friendships to the circle diagrams earlier in this chapter. Do you and your friends maintain separate and distinct individual identities while sharing your lives without wearing masks?
- Have you dealt with your "compulsion for completion" in the way God intended—by finding your personal identity and sense of meaning in God alone?
- Are you ready to take the risks involved in developing the kind of friendships that will change you, change others, and change the world?

Prayer

Loving Father, thank You for the gift of friendship. Help me to evaluate honestly the friendships in my life. Give me the insight to identify where I need to make changes. Grow my faith in You, Lord, so that I will have the strength of spirit to risk having the type of authentic friendships that this hurting world is longing for. Amen.

Three

Who Are You, Really?

The Futility of Living an Artificial Life

It's you I like.
—MISTER ROGERS

D o you like yourself?

I know, after discussing narcissism in an earlier chapter you might be hesitant to admit that you really do like yourself. Or maybe you're wondering what kind of boneheaded question this is. So let me ask it a different way.

When you lay your head on the pillow at night, what are your last thoughts before you drift off to sleep? Is it something like, *Lord, thank You for making me who I am. I'm honored that You chose to use me today in the lives of others. Thank You for giving my life meaning and eternal significance and for allowing me to help bring significance to the lives of others?*

Or is it more like this: *I have got to get to sleep. Why won't my mind stop racing? There's just too much to do. There is no way I can get everything done! It seems as though everybody wants a piece of me. But when do I ever get to do the things I really want to do? I wish I had some other life?*

Or maybe you try to fill your mind with noise, going to sleep with the television or radio playing. Or perhaps you bury your personal thoughts within a novel or some mental fantasy. Or maybe you take a sleeping pill or knock down a couple of nightcaps before retiring—anything to keep you from being alone with your own thoughts.

If you can't fall asleep thanking God for making you who you are and for using you in the lives of others, then think about what you don't like in yourself and why. This is crucial, because if you don't like yourself or your life, you can never authentically love others.

The core of true authenticity is to know *and* to be known; it is to love *and* to be loved. If you've decided not to like yourself, then you've decided, in effect, that you're unlikable. As a result, you will never allow others to get close enough to truly get to know you. Your fears will keep them at arm's length.

It's a common fear: "If they really got to know me, they'd just leave, and then I'd be alone." But think about this: if you don't let people get to know you, you're alone already.

LOVE IN A SWEATER AND TENNIS SHOES

Regardless of what you may think of Mister Rogers, your life has most likely been touched by him. Fred Rogers hosted the PBS show *Mister Rogers' Neighborhood* for more than thirty years, touching the lives of millions over three generations. His mission was simple: to make sure children (and even adults) knew that he liked them just the way they were. And he wanted them to like themselves too. Rogers understood the life-giving power of simply being liked.

In a university commencement address he delivered shortly before his death in 2002, Rogers made the following comments.

> For a long time I wondered why I felt like bowing when people showed their appreciation for the work that I've been privileged to do. What I've come to understand is that we who bow are probably—whether we know it or not—acknowledging the presence of the eternal: we're bowing to the eternal in our neighbor. You see, I believe that appreciation is a holy thing, that when we look for what's best in the person we happen to be with at the moment, we're doing what God does. So, in loving and appreciating our neighbor, we're participating in something truly sacred....
>
> I wonder if you've heard what happened at the Seattle Special Olympics a few years ago. For the 100-yard dash there were nine contestants...and at the sound of the gun they took off. But one little boy stumbled and fell and hurt his knee and began to cry. The other eight children heard the boy crying. They slowed down, turned around, saw the boy and ran back to him—every one of them ran back to him. One little girl with Down syndrome bent down and kissed the boy and said, "This will make it better."
>
> The little boy got up, and he and the rest of the runners linked their arms together and joyfully walked to the finish line.
>
> They all finished the race at the same time. And when they did, everyone in the stadium stood up and clapped and whistled and cheered.... Deep down we know that what matters in this life is much more than winning for ourselves. What really matters is helping others win, too, even if it means slowing down and changing our course now and then.[1]

What matters most to you? If you're honest with yourself—and if you haven't drowned out the deepest desires of your heart—it will be people. If you aren't honest—or if you don't really know who you are—you'll say your job matters the most, or status or achievement or even money. If people don't matter to you the most, can you honestly say that you like who you are?

THINKING ABOUT YOU

Allison had it all. She was pretty and smart, and she had a loving husband and two beautiful, healthy children. Her family lived in a house valued at three-quarters of a million dollars. The rock on her left hand could choke a Clydesdale. But there was one problem: she felt nothing—no love for her husband and no confidence that she was attractive. She found no joy in being a mother and felt little warmth toward her children. Sex with her husband was rote and obligatory. In daily life, she just felt nothing.

Interestingly, Allison didn't suffer from depression. It's true that she was gripped by melancholy. But she didn't need an antidepressant. She needed to like herself.

And then there is Bill, who in a therapy session voiced the real reason why he was struggling with accepting and loving his children. "I just hate *me!*" Bill announced. "And if you were me, you'd hate me too."

If you don't like yourself, it dominates your life. If you don't come to accept the person God made you to be, if you don't come to peace with the events of your past, then you will never be able to let someone else into your heart and soul. By not liking and accepting *you,* you will build a wall that keeps everyone and everything else away from you. And that wall—which promises protection but only traps you inside with your loneliness—will ultimately prevent you from experiencing life-changing love.

I don't advocate self-esteem as the answer to our ache. Being your own best friend won't work. You might remember the empty mantra of the irksome *Saturday Night Live* character Stuart Smalley: "Because I'm good enough, I'm smart enough, and doggone it...people like me!" He could never convince himself it was true.

Arrogance and pride can't make us likable—even to ourselves. Only the truth will open our eyes to our value. The apostle Paul described our worth: "If anyone is in Christ, he is a new creation; the old has gone, the new has come!" (2 Corinthians 5:17), and "You realize, don't you, that you are the temple of God, and God himself is present in you?" (1 Corinthians 3:16, MSG). And speaking as the "disciple whom Jesus loved," John exclaimed, "What marvelous love the Father has extended to us! Just look at it—we're called children of God! That's who we really are" (1 John 3:1, MSG).

There's no way around it. We are special to God. He's crazy about us. While He doesn't approve of all that we do, He really does like us. And while He wants us to like ourselves as new creations in Christ, we also are called to regard ourselves with "sober judgment" (Romans 12:3). Examining our lives with sober judgment involves dealing with the "me" who is loving—either authentically or artificially—others as well as ourselves.

ARTIFICIAL OR AUTHENTIC?

If you don't know who you are and why God has placed you here, you can't love others authentically. Likewise, if you don't like who you are, then you can't be effective at loving others authentically. We can't just settle for knowing in some abstract way that we need other people. We can't be satisfied with simply knowing that we need the right type of friends. We also need to be completely honest with ourselves and discover what type of friend we are to others.

Let's go back to Allison. She had all the things that are said to make a person happy and complete, and yet she found herself without feelings and without friends. The problem was not an inability to be friendly or a lack of contact with others. Rather, she believed that anyone who "pretended" to like her must want something from her. They must want her money or her house or even, as she thought about her husband's sexual appetite, her body. She assumed that her husband had proposed to her because of her looks, her ability to entertain others at parties, and even because her breasts were "much larger than average."

"I know they don't really like *me*," she confessed. "How could they? They don't know me. My husband doesn't even know me. If he knew what goes on in my head, he'd be at the lawyer's office before I could blink."

Allison's fear of being known and then rejected is a common malady. When I asked her about this fear, she knew exactly where it came from.

"I know they don't like me because I don't like myself. With all my junk, no one could like me. It's just easier to be nice to others, give them what they want, and just keep my own little world to myself."

It's safer to live that way, or at least it *seems* to be safer. Allison agreed with that observation. And when I suggested that it's also a much lonelier way to live, she reached for a tissue to wipe the tears that were pooling at the edges of her eyes.

"Maybe," she said. "But if I let someone get too close to me, I know they won't like what they find, and then they'll leave. And I will *really* be lonely. It's happened before."

Like the rest of us, Allison has been rejected and ostracized by others. At times in her past, people have made it known that they prefer to befriend others. She has been left out. She knows the pain of being alone.

We can choose one of two courses—only two. We can risk being hurt as we pursue real and authentic relationships with others. We may be rejected by a few people, and, yes, we'll feel lonely for a while until we pick ourselves up and pursue authenticity again. Or we can refuse to take the risk and keep ourselves closed off from others. If we choose that path, we *guarantee* our own loneliness—permanently.

"You're lonely either way," I told Allison. "Taking a risk—a huge risk—and knocking down the wall is the only way to end your loneliness." And the same is true for you.

DON'T SETTLE FOR BEING NICE

As a therapist and a pastor, I've known many people who think they can love others by being nice to them. They imagine they are bona fide friends to others because they do "nice things." These people are experts at being kind, but they despise themselves. They won't do the hard work of becoming whole apart from others, by finding their identity in who God made them to be. People who are entirely other-centered at the expense of self-awareness are, unknowingly, attempting to meet their own need for significance rather than trying to love their neighbor. They believe that by focusing on others and ignoring themselves they can be pleasing to God.

The truth is, God is not pleased, because it won't result in authentically loving others. The type of relationship that changes other people and brings an end to your own loneliness is not a one-way street. The type of relationship that brings comfort and peace involves knowing *and* being known, loving *and* being loved. It's impossible to love others while rejecting their love, because love requires a relationship. There must be a lover and, if you will, a lovee. And what's more, the lover must also be at times the lovee and vice versa.

God's essence is love (1 John 4:8), and He created us out of relationship—the love relationship that exists within the Trinity of Father, Son, and

45

Holy Spirit (see Genesis 1:26–27). The Trinity is, in fact, the perfect expression of relational intimacy. God is a relational Being, and He created us to be relational beings. That is part of what it means to bear the image of God.

God is the first and best Lover, and He initiated love toward us while we were still sinners (Romans 5:8). We were dead in our sins, and God chose to pursue us in relentless love. When we respond to that love, we are made alive in our spirits, and we can join God in changing the world through authentic relationships. We can now truly love others "because he first loved us" (1 John 4:19).

Why am I harping on this? Because this is the core of God's amazing, everyday solution to loneliness. He exists in the relationship of the Godhead, and He creates us to exist in relationship with Him and with one another. Without relationship there is no love, and without love there is loneliness. Authentic, naked-soul relationships end loneliness. Period.

If you refuse to give careful consideration to God's amazing love for you, there is no way that you can like yourself. But if you take to heart that God chose to love you, then how can you refuse to love yourself? If you conclude that you are ugly and unlovable, that you're imperfect and therefore unlikable, then you are calling God a liar. Remember, God loved us even when we were in full rebellion against Him (Romans 5:8).

How do we get past self-condemnation? It starts with getting alone and being quiet before God. We must view ourselves as God sees us. We must take to heart all that He has said about His love for us.

You have worth and are likable simply because God created you, God loves you, and God sacrificed His Son for you. God could not make a more forceful statement: you are inherently likable! He wants you to be at peace with who you are, accepting who you are and where you've been. In spite of the fact that we're all sinners and we've all done things we now regret, we need to live as precious children of our loving God. We do that by coming before the gracious God of the universe, seeking His forgiveness through Jesus Christ, and experiencing His love and mercy. Then we can live with the confidence that "long, long ago [God] decided to adopt us into his family through Jesus Christ. (What pleasure he took in planning this!)" (Ephesians 1:5, MSG).

What's not to like about that?

DON'T SETTLE FOR DOING YOUR DUTY

Remember Bill, the man who promised that if I were he, I would hate him too? He was one of his church's most reliable volunteers. He'd show up whenever people were needed to set up chairs or to help out with the youth group. He would gladly drive across town and back to pick up someone who needed a ride to church.

Bill was dutiful to a fault, but he would never let anyone else do anything for him. He gladly prayed for others but never asked others for prayer. He worried about how he was coming across, seeking always to make the best impression he could. But away from public view, Bill was slowly dying of a broken heart. He really did want to help others, but he cut himself off from the help he so desperately needed.

It's not hard to understand Bill's hurt. His parents divorced when he was young, after his dad had physically abused him. Bill started having sex at age fifteen, "getting whatever he could" from whatever girl would give it. And it didn't stop after he became an adult. He had an affair during his first year of marriage, one that he confessed to his wife. She forgave him, but Bill could never understand why she didn't show him the door. With all that he had done, how could *anyone* like him?

Then Bill came to faith in Christ. He and his wife had children, and he spent the next thirteen years trying to work off his debt to God and to the people he had wronged. But with each pat on the back, and with every "Bill, we are so blessed to have you around here," he died a little more inside.

"They don't know," he said. "They say these things only because they don't know me."

It's true that those around Bill didn't know him; they didn't know him because he didn't allow anyone to see inside his life. He was a dutiful church member and a tireless worker. But he was unwilling to take the risk of becoming real with those around him.

FROM ARTIFICIAL TO AUTHENTIC

Peter, one of Jesus's most famous disciples, was a yo-yo. He was impulsive and given to emotional outbursts. He often spoke before thinking, later regretting that he hadn't chosen his words more carefully. He could also speak the greatest truths and, unlike the others, take huge steps of faith. Peter could write the book on the victories and failures of life. But what he had going for him, and what kept him going, was a tremendous passion to know and follow Jesus.

Peter was a fisherman, a labor-intensive occupation that often produced little in exchange for much hard work. One morning, after Peter (then known as Simon) and his colleagues had worked all night with meager results, Jesus directed them to push out into deep water and let down their nets. Simon mentioned the futility of their past night's labor, but he followed Jesus's instructions anyway and soon caught so many fish that the nets began to break. Simon knew a miracle when he saw one, and it broke him.

But when Simon Peter saw that, he fell down at Jesus' feet, saying, "Go away from me Lord, for I am a sinful man, O Lord!"

For amazement had seized him and all his companions because of the catch of fish which they had taken; and so also were James and John, sons of Zebedee, who were partners with Simon. And Jesus said to Simon, "Do not fear, from now on you will be catching men." And when they had brought their boats to land, they left everything and followed Him. (Luke 5:8–11, NASB)

Bill, the dutiful church volunteer, needed a Simon experience. He needed to honestly and humbly confess that he was a sinner, as we all are. He needed to acknowledge that at times he did things that were hurtful to others and at times he was unlikable. Again, these things are true of all of us. And Bill needed to know that when we come face to face with Jesus, when our heart opens up and the "amazement" of His grace seizes us, our most appropriate response is to fall on our face and beg Jesus to depart from us, for we are fully aware of our sinfulness.

But remarkably, Jesus stays right there and says, "Do not fear." People who don't like themselves are paralyzed by the fear that someone will find out who they really are. And Jesus says, "Don't give in to that fear. I have a new life for you, a better life."

To be real for Christ, to be in a position to change the world by loving others in a way that matters, we must be real with ourselves. We must admit what is unlikable about us. We must bring it all before God and work to change what He puts His finger on. Then we must like the person we are and the person God is calling us to be—because God created us and called His creation "good." He created us because He wanted a relationship with us. He doesn't always love everything we do, but He is nuts about the people we are.

Getting right in our relationship with God—basing our security, worth, and identity on knowing Him and communing with Him—sets the stage for all the rest that follows in relationships.

How Great Are You, Really?

At the opposite end of the spectrum from those who don't like themselves are the people who think way too highly of themselves. Several years ago *U.S. News & World Report* published the results of a poll that asked Americans which celebrities and public figures they thought were "most likely to go to heaven." Here are some of the names that made the list, followed by the percentage of folks who thought these people would "likely" get past the Pearly Gates:

Mother Teresa, 79%

Oprah Winfrey, 66%

Michael Jordan, 65%

Colin Powell, 61%

Hillary Clinton, 55%

Al Gore, 55%

Bill Clinton, 52%

Pat Robertson, 47%

Newt Gingrich, 40%

Dennis Rodman, 28%

O. J. Simpson, 19%[2]

While you might question the level of support garnered by some of these celebrities, you were most likely not taken aback by the fact that Mother Teresa topped the list. That is until you hear that there was a vote-getter who ranked even higher. One individual amassed a confidence rating of 87 percent!

Who was this heaven-bound celebrity? It was the people who responded to the poll. They voted for *themselves*.

In fact, the survey respondents ranked their own chances of entering heaven ahead of Billy Graham. He wasn't even listed, at least in the report of the poll that I read.

Regardless of how you picture heaven, it's clear in Scripture that salvation and the forgiveness of our sins (which is our passport to God's presence) come by faith in Jesus Christ through His death and resurrection, not by faith in ourselves. There is no public-opinion poll that will make any difference.

The Bible says, "If you confess with your mouth, 'Jesus is Lord,' and believe in your heart that God raised him from the dead, you will be saved" (Romans 10:9). The Bible is also clear that our own good deeds—and our perception of ourselves—has nothing to do with it. "Saving is all his [God's] idea, and all his work. All we do is trust him enough to let him do it. It's God's gift from start to finish! We don't play the major role. If we did, we'd probably go around bragging that we'd done the whole thing!" (Ephesians 2:8–9, MSG).

Having sober judgment means knowing who we are in Christ. We are tainted by sin. We can't get into heaven by our own effort because we're not perfect. If we think we can get into heaven based on what we perceive to be good works or simply because we feel we're "a better person than most," we are deceived.

Even Jesus, who was perfect, was clearheaded in His view of Himself (see Philippians 2:6). He was God, of course, but His mission was to be a Servant. In His humility and because of His love, He gave up His place in heaven to endure the indignities of life on earth. And He did it for us. Now that's as authentic as you can get.

When you lay your head on your pillow at night, do you know you need God? And do you know that He loves you so much that He provided the path to get you into His presence, into heaven itself?

Sober judgment means not just accepting but *liking* the place where God has put you. It means liking the gifts He has given you, the tasks He has called you to do, and even the body that He created for you to use on earth. God allows us the freedom to make our own choices. We can choose to relish the work God has given us to do, or we can spend our time trying to do what *we* think is important.

God wants us to change the world by loving others authentically and letting them love us the same way. Our problem is that we often get caught up in what those around us think is important—and what they think of us. In place of loving and being loved, we think our happiness and fulfillment will come by making ourselves more important in the eyes of others. When we dislike our place in the world, and when we don't know who we are and what God has called us to do, we end up using and even abusing others.

Don't Be a Chicken

In the 1920s a group of biologists conducted what has come to be known as the Pecking Order study. The scientists studied how chickens established dominance in the barnyard. (Trust me, it relates to what we're talking about.) They noted that every hen had a definite place in the hierarchy. The chicken's position in relation to others allowed her either to "peck" at those below her or demanded that the hen had to allow herself to be pecked by those above her. For you nonfarmer types, chickens can be vicious. If a certain chicken suffered a small wound that drew blood, that chicken was in imminent danger of being pecked to death. By getting a chicken "out of the way," so to speak, other hens got to move up in rank.[3]

This pecking-order view of the world is avidly practiced among humans, and it can be as vicious as the barnyard version. Pastor Bill Hybels notes that we often treat people we perceive to be above us in the social order with honor and respect, while we treat those below us with disdain. He states that we laud rock stars, renowned athletes, and other celebrities as if fame makes them special. We treat janitors, waiters, and other "unknowns" as if they're our personal servants. If we're sitting at our desk when the boss happens to come in, we have all the time in the world. We even ask him or her, "What can I do for you?" But if we're working late, and the custodian comes in to empty the trash, we bark, "Can't you come back later so you won't interrupt my work?"

We've all been guilty of catering to those who have the power to move us up in the pecking order. But the Bible makes it clear that sucking up will keep us from living an authentic life.

> My dear friends, don't let public opinion influence how you live out our glorious, Christ-originated faith. If a man enters your church wearing an expensive suit, and a street person wearing rags comes in right after him, and you say to the man in the suit, "Sit here, sir; this is the best seat in the house!" and either ignore the street person or say, "Better sit here in the back row," haven't you segregated God's children and proved that you are judges who can't be trusted?
>
> Listen, dear friends. Isn't it clear by now that God operates quite differently? He chose the world's down-and-out as the kingdom's first citizens, with full rights and privileges. This kingdom is promised to anyone who loves God. And here you are abusing these same citizens! (James 2:1–6, MSG)

I can't tell you the particular plan God has for your life. I don't know where you think you fall in the pecking order. But I can tell you this: your place in the world—and my place in this world—is to authentically love other people, regardless of their place.

DIRECTIONS FROM INSIDE

Have you ever noticed that almost everything in the advertising world is designed to make us *not* like ourselves? Just about everything being sold promises to make us thinner, better looking, healthier, and basically a lot happier. "If I just go on that Caribbean cruise, then I'll be happy. Yeah, that's the ticket. And if I had that SUV, that look, and even that girl, and a full head of hair, man, *then* I'd be happy." It's good to mock the idiocy of the advertising world that tries to make us hate our life. But there are too many people who don't separate reality from the fantasy of advertising.

In the 1950s, sociologist David Riesman argued that there were two basic kinds of people—other-directed people and inner-directed people.[4] Other-directed people take their sense of being and even their sense of direction for life from those they are around. At the extreme, other-directed people are chameleons, going along with whatever the crowd is doing because they don't want to be thought of as different. They gossip when others are gossiping, they turn religious around a church group, and they even stand on desks and throw spit wads because of their buddies.

Not only are other-directed people easily influenced, they also are experts at using other people for their own advancement. They divide others into two categories: those from whom they can get something and those they are careful to avoid. If they can't use another person for their own benefit, they become hypervigilant in assessing how that person acts toward them. When they are hurt by others, they protect themselves and vow they won't be hurt again. When others cause them pain, other-directed people simply act as though they don't care. As they get older, they develop softer and softer skin, but harder and harder hearts.

Inner-directed people, on the other hand, derive their sense of purpose from within. They know who they are and are authentic to who they are, no matter whom they are with. Pecking orders are meaningless to these people. In computer terms, they are WYSIWYG: what you see is what you get. And one more thing: they like who they are.

It is the inner-directed people who know their purpose: to know and be known, to love and be loved. They strive to maintain and improve relationships by seeking forgiveness and reconciliation whenever possible. They care about what other people think and do, but in a constructive way. If the actions of others cause pain, they seek, with God's help, not to respond selfishly but rather with love and grace. They seek reconciliation. As they get older, they develop tougher skin and softer hearts.

Inner-directed people reject the lies of our culture, while other-directed people accept the lies and learn to hate the person that God created them to be. Taking your cues from those around you will lead to the pursuit of approval and acceptance, rather than living to love others and to be loved by them. Not only will you not change the world, you'll never escape the pain and loneliness of your own world.

Over time, you'll forget that it's real love you were longing for in the first place.

THE COST OF LOVE

There's another person I want you to meet. I'll call her Abby, and I have her permission to tell her story. I met Abby almost twenty years ago when I was the youth director at her church. She hated the fact that her parents fought all the time. She hated the fact that she felt so alone and that nobody really cared about the pain she suffered. She hated herself. She hated life.

And on more than one occasion she hated it enough to attempt suicide.

But God's love broke through in the form of a friend who simply and powerfully loved Abby just as she was. The friend saw the worst but knew the best was yet to come. The friend loved her enough to break down the walls and prove to Abby that she was likable, even lovable, and that God and many others were absolutely crazy about her.

Twenty years ago Abby wrote this poem for me, and I cherish it to this day. It shows the power of being authentic, even in pain and loneliness.

How Much Does It Cost?

I don't think I ever really wanted to go;
There was just so much pain,
I wanted someone to know.

As I look into those eyes I realized there was someone
who did care;
Understanding my pain;
Understanding that life wasn't fair.

I was just a kid trying desperately to escape.
I didn't want to go,
But what choice could I make?

I just wanted to feel loved and not feel so lost.
I wanted someone to hold on to;
How much does it cost?[5]

How much does it cost to feel loved? It costs taking the risk of letting someone inside your heart. It costs the strength and will to look in the mirror and change what needs to be changed and to accept what does not. It costs the fear of breaking out of a me-centered world, knowing that I need others, and doing the hard work of becoming whole with God first so I can then be authentic with other people.

How much does it cost to feel loved?

It cost God His only Son.

WHAT MATTERS MOST

Do you like yourself? Do you know who you are? Do you know why you're here?

The Bible makes clear who we are and why we're here: "For we are God's workmanship, created in Christ Jesus to do good works, which God prepared in advance for us to do" (Ephesians 2:10). The only honest answer to the question "Who are you?" is that you are God's magnificent creation, His *very best* workmanship. The honest answer to "Why are you here?" is that you are created to carry out the greatest work of all: to authentically love other people and to be loved by them (see 1 Corinthians 13:13).

And that, as Mister Rogers would say, is what matters most.

Reflection

The Big Idea

God is absolutely, positively crazy about you. And as you exercise sober judgment, He wants you to examine your life and commit to putting away falsehood and putting on authenticity. And get this: He wants you to be extremely thankful that you are who you are. You are His creation, and it doesn't get any better than that!

Key Verse

"For we are God's workmanship, created in Christ Jesus to do good works, which God prepared in advance for us to do." (Ephesians 2:10)

Answering Questions

- In your heart of hearts, as you lay your head on your pillow at night, are you at peace with who you are? Are you able to thank God for making you the person you are today?
- Have you been guilty of seeing your place in the world in the context of a human pecking order? Do you make decisions regarding your life as an inner-directed person or an other-directed person? What changes do you feel God wants you to make?
- Are you ready to live for what matters most? Are you ready to do the hard work of finding out who you are as God's creation and then living in the world as the person God made you to be?

Prayer

Gracious Lord, You are the Creator of all life. You have given me my heart, my soul, and my body. Yet it's so hard at times to be thankful for who I am. Forgive me, Father, for criticizing Your work. Forgive me as well for the times I have thought too highly of myself. Help me to see myself as You see me—as Your adopted child, as a person created to do good works for You. May I learn to live my life every day as an offering to you. Amen.

Four

Do You Love God?

Answering Life's Most Dangerous Question

Do, or do not. There is no try.

—YODA

o you love God? The quick and easy answer is, "Of course." Then you can just move on.

Too bad it's not that simple.

Think about the words for a moment. Do you love *God?* If you answered no, then nothing in this book will prove true in your life. But if you answered, "Yes, I do love God," then you must ask yourself a second question: "How is my life different from the person who answers no?"

It's comforting to think about God's love for us. Our souls can find rest and reassurance in the scriptures that speak of the Shepherd who would leave ninety-nine sheep to pursue the one that gets lost or the Father who welcomes back the prodigal son with open arms and even runs to greet the lost son while he is still on the road. But how does my life demonstrate the outward results of my loving God?

Thinking about my love for God is not safe; it is risky. "Do you love God?" can be the most dangerous question we'll ever try to answer.

GOD AND AUTHENTICITY

If you're wondering how the question of loving God fits into the discussion of loving other people authentically and why it is such a dangerous question, look at some verses that describe what loving God looks like.

Jesus said:

> If anyone loves me, he will obey my teaching. My Father will love him, and we will come to him and make our home with him. He who does not love me will not obey my teaching. (John 14:23–24)

And:

> Whoever has my commands and obeys them, he is the one who loves me. He who loves me will be loved by my Father, and I too will love him and show myself to him. (John 14:21)

Love and obedience are wrapped together. If we love God, we'll obey Jesus's teachings. And when we do, Jesus reveals Himself to us. But love and obedience aren't easy. Loving God means doing what He asks—including the risky things.

Take Jeremy, one of my old seminary classmates. He was a twenty-two-year-old recent college graduate, like me, who was immersed in the world of theological academia, trying to figure out the best way to serve God. But Jeremy, also like me, was attending seminary far from his home base. So when he wasn't engaged in discussions of systematic theology and Greek verb conjugation, he was lonely. But instead of sharing his need with classmates or professors who could provide healthy personal relationships, he started hitting bars and strip clubs on the far side of town. He also began dating women he met in his off-campus job. I can tell you that he wasn't interested in these women for captivating intellectual or spiritual conversations. He was starving for physical contact. Some of the women he kissed, others he fondled, and still others he took to bed.

Jeremy knew he was using these women for his own selfish gratification. And he usually felt guilty about it afterward. As a pastor in training, he realized he was violating his love relationship with Jesus by disobeying His teachings.

But for brief moments, as he sat in a bar or a strip club or as he pursued yet another available co-worker, he experienced some relief from the ache of loneliness. Then he'd have to drive back to the seminary, where he'd feel more alone than ever. He was pretending to love God while rejecting the obedience demanded by that love. He was using his neighbor, not loving his neighbor.

Jeremy knew that God is a God of grace and forgiveness. But he also knew that eventually he'd have to deal with the voice in his spirit that said, "If you love Me, you will obey My commands."

WHERE LOVING BEGINS

Where does loving God and obeying Him start? Jesus said whenever we do good for "one of the least of these brothers of mine, you [do the same] for me" (Matthew 25:40). The apostle John drove this point home: "Anyone who does not love his brother, whom he has seen, cannot love God, whom he has not seen" (1 John 4:20). We love God by loving our neighbor. Conversely, we're not loving God if we refuse to love our neighbor.

John also said, "If anyone says, 'I love God,' yet hates his brother, he is a liar" (1 John 4:19). Liar or lover? What are we? Now the question of whether we love God becomes a very dangerous question indeed.

Jesus even put the question of loving God in the context of hating those who are closest to us. "If anyone comes to me and does not hate his father and mother, his wife and children, his brothers and sisters—yes, even his own life—he cannot be my disciple" (Luke 14:26). Do you sense the danger now?

We know from understanding biblical languages that Jesus was not referring to the first definition of *hate* found in *Webster's:* "to have a great aversion to, with a strong desire that evil should befall the person toward whom the feeling is directed." Rather it is the third definition, "to love less, relatively," that captures the core of what Christ is saying.[1] In context, to "hate" one's father and mother and wife and family—and self—means to care less about them than we do about Christ. To love God means to love Him more than all others. We must put God first.

God is the One who lovingly calls your name and asks you to come to Him, the One who, as Max Lucado points out, will rise and applaud for you as you enter heaven, the One who loved *you* so much that He sent His one and only Son to die for you.[2] In response to His overwhelming love for you, is He the primary voice you listen to? Is His Word the blueprint for your life? Do your actions demonstrate the love of God regardless of how others may view such devotion? Is He your only true Master?

If we want authentic relationships that will change the world, then we have to honestly evaluate what loving God means in daily life. And the place to begin loving God above all else is to love your neighbor.

BACK TO THE BASICS

So just who is my neighbor?

Fred Rogers always opened his television show, *Mister Rogers' Neighborhood*, (like I need to tell you) with a musical question: "Would you be my neighbor?" As I think about it now, I don't believe that's how Jesus would start the show. He would ask, "Are you *being* a neighbor?"

The answer to the question "Who is my neighbor?" is not based on whether someone *agrees* to be my neighbor. When a self-serving lawyer asked the neighbor question to Jesus, the answer came in the form of a story. If Jesus were telling the story today, it might sound something like this:

A man sat alone, slumped over on the dirty sidewalk, leaning against the cold brick building next to the alley. He held his knees close to his chest in a vain attempt to keep warm. He was unwashed, thoroughly disheveled— a street person. A continuous parade of people hurried past in both directions. The man would occasionally mutter, "Excuse me. Can you spare a little change?"

A well-heeled investment banker came walking by and, understanding the economics of the poor, simply hurried on, casting a disapproving glance at the man. *They have shelters for these people,* he thought.

Next, a teacher approached with a small group of students in tow on their way to the symphony. It was a cultural field trip, but the homeless man was not the cultural experience the teacher was looking for. She quickly found a crosswalk and hurried the students across the street.

An elder at a large suburban church approached next. He knew that he should take the man around the corner to a sandwich shop, but he also knew he was running late to an important appointment. He decided he couldn't spare the time, and he had been taught never just to give money. He, too, quickly passed by, vowing he would take the man to lunch the next time he saw him.

Finally a teenager approached. Her hair was dyed three different colors and cut in geometric shapes. Tattoos of dragons covered her arms, and her nose, lips, and brows were cluttered with metal piercings. She was dressed in black, hurrying to meet her boyfriend who had threatened to leave her behind if she showed up late. But when she saw the man, her heart broke. She knew about hunger, and she knew about being ignored. All she had was ten dollars, and if her boyfriend left without her, she would need the money to get back home. But still, she couldn't ignore the hungry man. It hurt her to know that he had to live that way. She took the money out of her pocket, handed it to the man, smiled, and said, "I hope this helps."[3]

Who was the neighbor to this man?

God wants us to help those in need, to be inconvenienced for the sake of others. In Jesus's version of this parable, the one who helped the man was a Samaritan, a member of a mixed race of Jewish and Gentile heritage despised by most orthodox Jews. (I say "most" because Christ certainly didn't share this bias.) The important "religious people" of the day passed by the hurt man. It was the despised Samaritan who loved God by coming to the aid of his neighbor.

The Samaritan didn't love out of obligation but out of compassion and a broken heart. Before he took the injured man to receive care for his wounds, the Samaritan "saw the man's condition [and] *his heart went out to him*" (Luke 10:33, MSG). He acted on the man's behalf because he truly did love his neighbor. The proof was the softness and kindness of his heart.

The question that prompted this parable was asked by a lawyer. He asked Jesus, "Who is my neighbor?" But before that, he had asked,

"Teacher, what do I need to do to get eternal life?" (Luke 10:25, MSG). Before giving *the* answer, Christ asked the legal expert what he thought the answer was. The man replied, "'Love the Lord your God with all your heart and with all your soul and with all your strength and with all your mind'; and, 'Love your neighbor as yourself'" (Luke 10:27). He actually got the answer right, at least in the beginning.

Then Jesus turned the tables. The lawyer was now answering questions—questions about what he believed and how he lived. And he was starting to squirm. He wanted Jesus to say that his comfortable, safe life was pleasing to God. He wanted to hold on to the life he already had, with neighbors of his own choosing.

But I would bet that as soon as he answered Jesus's question with the words, "You shall love the Lord your God...and love your neighbor as yourself," he knew he was trapped. This man, who had spent his life studying *about* God, began to realize that living according to the words of Scripture, living *for* God, was dangerous. No longer was mere knowledge good enough. He was being told by the Master Teacher, "Do you love your neighbor? If you do, you'll know that your neighbor is all people, especially those in need."

Neighbors are all around us.

And there's one more thing to notice in this story. Jesus did not define the neighbor from an egocentric perspective. In other words, He did not define neighbors according to their proximity to the person asking the question. Instead, Jesus asked, "Who was the neighbor to the man in need?" Christ was interested in who *acted* like a neighbor to the person in need.[4]

More than asking, "Who is my neighbor?" we should ask, "Am I *being* a neighbor to those who need me?" That will begin to answer the question, "Do you love God?"

HYPERINDIVIDUALISM

In summarizing survey findings regarding the religious beliefs and practices of those aged twenty to twenty-nine, researcher David Kinnaman (himself a twenty-something) states that even though less than one-third of men and women in that age range attend church in any given week, their reasons for questioning the importance and relevance of church are legitimate.

> Their disenchantment has raised questions for churches
> related to relevance, discipleship, authenticity, the use of art
> and technology in ministry, relationships, music, learning
> styles and teaching, teamwork, leadership hierarchy, stewardship,
> and much more. On the flip side of the coin, young adults—
> many who have grown up in unhealthy families—struggle
> with character issues, with relational isolation brought on
> by their hyper-individualism, with Bible familiarity, and with
> being over-critical of their elders. Consequently, many of the
> legitimate questions young leaders ask get lost in the jumble
> of generational warfare.[5]

What strikes me most about Kinnaman's analysis is that, due in part to unhealthy family backgrounds, many twenty-somethings struggle with relational isolation brought on by "hyperindividualism." A generation bred in the crucible of shattered relationships places an extremely high value on "being the very best person that you can be for your own success in life." What gets lost on this individualistic path is real, authentic relationships.

While individualism focuses on self-development, it leaves us lonely. At everybody's core is a yearning deeper than the drive to succeed. Our core yearning is for realness in our relationships. By pursuing our individual wants, we guarantee our own loneliness. And we also fail to demonstrate our love for God because, in effect, we are ignoring the true needs of others.

LOOKING OUT FOR ME

As I was writing this chapter, I took my lovely bride to an island off the coast of Florida to celebrate our wedding anniversary. We loved the quiet, no-cars, get-away-from-it-all atmosphere. We love our three kids, but we also crave uninterrupted time with just each other.

As I enjoyed time with Amy, I was reading a John Grisham novel, which seemed to be the book God wanted me to read as I wrote this chapter. The story is about a young lawyer, Michael Brock, who with a few fellow lawyers is taken hostage by a homeless man. There are indications that the hostage taker, known as "Mister," is less concerned about a ransom than he is about bringing attention to people's greed.

One of Mister's tactics is to review the tax returns of the lawyers locked in the conference room. After the 1040s are faxed in, Mister has Brock get his own return and asks, "How much did you give away last year?" Deciding it would not be wise to lie, Brock answers.

> "I gave a thousand dollars to Yale," I said. "And two thousand to
> the local United Way."
> "How much did you give to poor people?"
> I doubted if the Yale money went to feed needy students.
> "Well, the United Way spreads the money around the city, and
> I'm sure some of it went to help the poor."
> "How much did you give to the hungry?"

"I paid fifty-three thousand dollars in taxes, and a nice chunk of it went for welfare, Medicaid, aid to dependent children, stuff like that."

"And you did this voluntarily, with a giving spirit?"

"I didn't complain," I said, lying like most of my countrymen.

"Have you ever been hungry?"

…"No," I said, "I have not."

"Have you ever slept in the snow?"

"No."

"You make a lot of money, yet you're too greedy to hand me some change on the sidewalk." He waved the gun at the rest of them. "All of you. You walk right by me as I sit and beg. You spend more on fancy coffee than I do on meals. Why can't you help the poor, the sick, the homeless? *You have so much.*"[6]

We can come up with plenty of reasons why we don't give to those in need: They'll only spend it on drugs or booze; giving will only keep them on the street; they're just lazy. Various approaches have been recommended to really help the homeless, including taking the person to get a hot meal to assure that he doesn't settle for a bottle of wine. But that approach takes a lot more time than simply handing a street person a dollar bill. We typically don't help at all because we "don't have the time right now."

But I have so much.

I think of all of the times I've passed the same man on the corner of Washington Street and Illinois in downtown Indianapolis. He plays his saxophone with his case open in front of him. I have walked to the next corner before crossing to his side of the street, to avoid having to walk past him. I think of the elderly man in the beat-up overcoat whom I occasionally see sitting by the alleyway a half block south of Monument Circle (a top tourist attraction in town). He holds a cup for change, and I glance the other direction as if I'm checking traffic so I can cross the street.

I reflect on all the times I've passed people like the saxophonist and the man by the alley, hurrying to get back to "important" business, not sparing a dime. And yet later that same day I don't give a second thought to paying three dollars for a stupid cup of coffee.

I must ask myself, "Do I love God?" I have so much!

IF WE LOVE, WE MUST DO

The apostle John wrote, "This is love for God: to obey his commands. And his commands are not burdensome" (1 John 5:3). Jesus said, "Do you want to know the two most important things God said we are to do if we want to follow Him? Do you want to know the traits your life should reflect if you deeply love God? Here they are.

> The first in importance is, "Listen, Israel: The Lord your God is one; so love the Lord God with all your passion and prayer and intelligence and energy." And here is the second: "Love others as well as you love yourself." (Mark 12:29–31, MSG)

We all know that Jesus would not cross the street to avoid a needy person. He wouldn't engage in an internal debate over the needy spending the money on liquor or smokes or drugs. He wouldn't donate a helpful suggestion rather than a few dollars. After all, street people already know where the rescue mission is.

It does no good to rationalize with thoughts like, *Jesus lived in a different time. He was not as busy as I am. Plus, it was His job to help the poor and homeless. I already have a very demanding job!* James said if we see someone in need and do nothing but tell the person, "Go, I wish you well; keep warm and well fed," without doing anything to help the person's physical needs, then what we have done is worthless (James 2:16).

Jesus ministered to each individual at his or her point of deepest hurt. In His divinity, Jesus knew each person's greatest need. But our not being divine is not an excuse for us to avoid loving others. We already know each person's greatest need, and that is to know Christ.

I have a neighbor who belongs to a cult that denies many of the basic truths about God's grace. They gather every Saturday morning for neighborhood canvassing—in other neighborhoods, it turns out. My neighbor is friendly. We chat and loan tools to each other. Our children play together. It's easy for me to be judgmental about his confused and misplaced faith. It is too easy for me to believe that he will *never* come to the light of Jesus Christ, because he is so blinded by false teaching.

Maybe I'm the one who is blind. Can't I see my neighbor's need? Maybe I'm the one who is prideful. Don't I know that I am a beggar too and that sharing the gospel is simply one beggar telling another beggar where to find food? Maybe I'm the one who, even though I *say* I believe the right things, actually lives under false teachings that say, "My neighbor is so bound up in deception, he could never hear the truth. He would never respond to Jesus's message of grace."

Never? Jesus wouldn't fall for this self-deception.

We have so much. And what we have the most of are the "unsearchable riches of Christ" (Ephesians 3:8). I need to have people pray for me the way Paul prayed for the Ephesians: "I pray also that the eyes of your heart may be enlightened in order that you may know the hope to which he has called you, the riches of his glorious inheritance in the saints, and his incomparably great power for us who believe" (Ephesians 1:18–19).

We have hope; we have a glorious inheritance; we have incomparably great power. We do have so much.

Every day we're surrounded by needy neighbors. Every day we have the choice of helping or doing nothing. People who have plenty of food and adequate shelter still have crying needs. They need a friend, a listening ear, a gentle touch, a kind word. And we're busy, hurried, preoccupied, it's true. But what should you do about the child your son befriended, the kid whose father is married to another woman and living in a different city and who always seems to be hanging out at your house? The child is hungry for a caring adult to show some interest in his life. What should you do?

Feeling guilty is not the point, nor is it my purpose in asking these questions. My hope and my prayer is that we will be convinced that "God can do anything, you know—far more than you could ever imagine or guess or request in your wildest dreams! He does it not by pushing us around but by working within us, his Spirit deeply and gently within us" (Ephesians 3:20, MSG). I pray that we will know in every fiber of our being that "God did not give us a spirit of timidity, but a spirit of power, of love and of self-discipline. [As such, we need] not be ashamed to testify about our Lord" (2 Timothy 1:7–8).

We need never be ashamed to love God by loving others.

START PRAYING

Do you want a life with meaning? Do you want to experience true authenticity in your relationships—with yourself, with others, and with God? Do you want to be an agent of God's amazing, everyday answer to loneliness?

Then pray to fall in love with God more and more. We can't have loneliness-ending, naked-soul relationships without loving God, and we can't genuinely experience God's love in a world-altering way without keeping

His commandments. And that begins with loving your neighbor—all your neighbors.

Remember my friend Jeremy—the seminary-trained pastor who used others in an effort to block out his loneliness? He eventually tired of leading a double life. He slowly realized he needed to simply and profoundly fall in love with Jesus. He learned to be real. He learned to reach out to others. He learned that, even though we are all sinners and we all fail, loving God means obeying God. And he learned that in reaching out to his neighbor, his own loneliness vanished. And remember me? I no longer walk by people on the street without doing something.

We must pray daily that God will empower us to live a life that reflects and demonstrates our love for Him. Pray to fall in love with God. Pray that God will make you color-blind, weight-blind, status-blind, power-blind, those-who-can-benefit-you-blind, money-blind, beauty-blind, you're-not-my-type-blind, intelligence-blind, cool-blind, what-about-me?-blind, you're-too-needy-blind. Pray that your heart may go out to your neighbor.

You and I have so much…

Reflection

The Big Idea
If we truly love God, we will do what He asks us to. If we do what He asks, then we will love our neighbor and that love will be demonstrated in action. We can't say we love God and then ignore our neighbor's needs. We are to be lovers, not liars.

Key Verse
"If anyone loves me, he will obey my teaching. My Father will love him, and we will come to him and make our home with him." (John 14:23)

Answering Questions

- How do you answer life's most dangerous question: Do you love God? What are the ramifications for your life and your relationships? What benefits have you seen from loving God by loving others?
- Are you willing to examine your life prayerfully and ask God to reveal areas where you are falling short of keeping His commandments?
- Are you ready to demonstrate your love for God by loving the people He brings into your life? Name one or two people whose needs you have been made aware of. Share with a close friend your commitment to love others, and ask your friend to hold you accountable.

Prayer

Gracious Lord, Your love for me is so vast it's impossible for me to fully comprehend it. Yet it is Your love that gives me the ability to love others. You have called me to love You by obeying You, and that includes loving the people around me.

Help me, Lord, to love You completely. May my life reflect the One who created love. May my life honor You. Amen.

Five

Losing Friends in the Red Zone

The Relational Threat of a Hurried Life

I'm in a hurry and don't know why.

—THE MUSIC GROUP ALABAMA

A re you in a hurry? Can you slow down long enough to answer?

Given the pace of life, I applaud the fact that you are taking time to read this book, or at least this chapter. Well, at least this paragraph. Or perhaps you insist that you're *not* in a hurry. You're just a regular person, doing life like everyone else.

Think about this: When approaching a stoplight, do you move to the lane with the fewest cars in line? At the grocery store, do you count the number of people in *every* line, estimate the combined number of items in their carts, and then calculate which line will move fastest? Once you commit to a line, do you keep track of the line you almost got in, just to check where you would have been had you selected that line? And then if your line slows down, do you get really ticked? At a bank drive-through with an equal number of cars in each lane, do you park in the *middle* so you can move to the lane that opens first? Do you get upset with people who *don't* have answering machines?

Do I need to go on?

You might be reading this because someone who cares about you sensed you were living in life's red zone and could benefit from slowing down. By now you're starting to skim this section, getting just enough to prove to your friend that you read it. Or perhaps you picked up this book out of desperation because you sense that living life at full speed is robbing you of anything authentic in life—including the relationships you long for. Either way, please read on—slowly.

In February 1964, *Life* magazine looked into the future and declared: "The task ahead: how to take life easy."[1] With the onslaught of new household gadgetry, many people believed that the biggest problem facing Americans in the future would be a glut of leisure time. What were we going to do with our new, slow-paced life?

Well, what are you doing with your glut of free time?

Gadgets or not, we're now moving faster than ever. Most of us experience frequent bouts of a disease called "hurry sickness." It is beyond epidemic. Still, many of us maintain the grinding pace because we believe it's necessary to get ahead, or at least to avoid falling behind. Many of us are sick but in denial.

Even sadder is the relational cost of this sickness. If you want another truth you can hang your proverbial hat on, here it is: you will never experience heart-healing, naked-soul relationships if you're living in the red zone. Hurry disease will rob you of love, and it will rob you of life.[2]

SPEEDAHOLICS AREN'T ANONYMOUS

The fact that we live much of our lives on the edge of mental and physical exhaustion is not news. But if you still doubt that it's a real problem, consider the physical and emotional destruction that occur when we live life at a breakneck pace. Writing about hurry sickness in a magazine geared for pastors and other church leaders, author and pastor John Ortberg (and the one to whom I owe many of these insights) describes the symptoms of this relationship-crippling disease.[3] People infected with hurry sickness often find their lives plagued by the following behaviors:

Speeding up. There is never enough time to get everything done. We get depressed or angry when something that is designed to accelerate our day gets sidetracked—a shortcut to an appointment ends up taking longer; you spill your travel mug of coffee and have to clean up the mess.

Multitasking. We praise those who are experts at doing many things at once. Management training seminars explain how it's done. The problem is that multitasking is not just a description of a particular skill set; it can be a sign of a rushed life and disordered heart.

This is not to say that life doesn't sometimes call for multitasking. Mothers of preschoolers are the true masters of this skill, but for them it's a necessity, not an obsession. The problem comes when we begin to feel we *have* to multitask simply to get through the day. We have to read while watching television while paying bills while checking our kids' homework. Can you sit in a restaurant by yourself and enjoy a meal, or do you need to be reading business reports? To teens and twenty-somethings, polyphasic activity (the psychological term for multitasking) has become the norm. They instant message while they write a paper for school while they do research on the Internet while they watch TV while they eat dinner while listening to music. We're getting more skilled at juggling, but where's our peace? Where's our ordered heart?

Clutter. Clutter is a hurry-sick problem when the person buried in the clutter is constantly longing for simplicity and the day when he or she will finally get organized. Clutter is a hurry-sick problem when you are constantly buying the latest "get organized" gadget, magazine, or planner. Being hurried creates clutter, if nowhere else but in our hearts.

SOLD ON SPEED

We no longer have time to be patient. We've begun to measure life by what author Robert Levine calls the shortest measurement of time: the honko-second. That is the amount of time that lapses between a traffic light's turning green and the driver of the second car in line laying on the horn.[4] We are honko-second people.

Our culture applauds hurry. *USA Today* reported: "Taking a cue from Domino's success formula, a Detroit hospital guarantees that emergency room patients will be seen within twenty minutes—or treatment is free." According to the story, the hospital's market share rose 30 percent following this campaign.[5] We buy fast and avoid slow. Trouble is, relationships often fall into the "slow" category. Authenticity takes time. But since time is such a rare commodity, real relationships become optional. Things get done, but friendships suffer.

A twenty-six-year-old professional woman told me, "I *always* feel in a rush no matter where I am or what I'm doing. There are some nights when I can't sleep because I'm stressing over the next day and how I won't have enough time to do what I need to do.... Sometimes, I make working out or other superficial items more of a priority than friends."

In my counseling work, I often help busy (and rushed) executives of all ages achieve balance between their work and their nonwork lives. And it seems that the twenty-something crowd has perfected hurry sickness. They are the first generation born with it. After their parents developed it in the 1970s and 1980s, it was bred into them. Is it any wonder that this age group is more lonely, more depressed, and more stressed out than any generation before?

We *all* need to be immersed in Jesus's model for a sane pace in life. Is there any record that He ever rebuked a person for moving too slowly? Did He ever appear in a hurry, even on the way to see someone who was dying? No, for Jesus there is this kindness and compassion thing. And there is also that thing about loving my neighbor as myself. Pastor and author Bill Hybels has observed that many of us are quick to talk about being God's agents of mercy on earth, but when we get in the car we are transformed into God's instrument of judgment.[6]

We don't need to quote the studies that cite how phenomenally few minutes parents spend each day in real conversation with their children or how long it's been since the average married couple had a date out by themselves. We know we're in a hurry, or at least we'd know it if we ever stopped long enough to reflect on our lives.

OH YEAH? WELL, WALK A MILE IN *MY* SHOES

I can hear the cry of many: "But you don't understand my situation!" I can hear it because I'm saying it myself. But as the words ring in my head, I remember that it's a voice that I've tried very hard to silence. It's the voice that tells me I'm worth very little unless I'm doing something big and doing it with dispatch. That voice is *not* God's voice.

Which voice do you believe?

Hurry sickness has spawned the notion that if we are doing something, we are important. Our existence is justified when we are performing some activity. How did we ever look ourselves in the mirror before we had the added productivity made possible by pagers, cell phones, overnight delivery, and e-mail? Likewise, how did we get to the place where we felt guilty just sitting and doing nothing?

Hurry is wrong, deadly in fact, because it kills relationships.

A few years ago I began to reflect on how I wanted my children to remember me after they grow up. I decided that when my children are asked, as adults, "What were some of your dad's favorite sayings?" I didn't want their first answer to be, "Hurry up and get in the van!" Back then, the van phrase was almost my personal mantra: "How come you're not in the van? Get your shoes on and get in the van!" Hurry sickness is a learned behavior. I don't want my children learning it from me.

Another experiment I tried was simply to avoid using the word *busy.* Sounds easy enough, but it's not. A big reason is because *busy* is a word we use automatically. Someone asks, "Hey, how are you?" And we say, "Busy!" People even open conversations with, "How are you? Busy, I bet!" Why are they so sure? It's almost as if they want to pay me a compliment by recognizing how preoccupied I am.

To help change this mind-set, when people now ask me how I'm doing, I try to answer with a few details about my life. If they ask about my kids, I try to describe their mental and spiritual state (or their hormone state) and not their activity list. If someone inquires of my lovely wife, I simply sing her praises (which can be a *very* long conversation).

Go ahead. Try to avoid using the *b* word.

Why do I tell my children before bedtime: "Pick out a *quick* book tonight!" Why do I say, "*Hurry* upstairs and get ready for bed?" Will an extra five minutes in a little longer book really destroy my schedule? Will it matter in the scope of eternity?

Yes it will. It will matter for the good of eternity and the future of my relationship with my children. I will either teach them that accomplishment and activity are what's most important and that, frankly, I don't have time to be with them, or I can teach the opposite lesson, the one with eternal significance. I can show them how vitally important it is simply to "be" with them. It is my experience, as a father and a counselor, that our reasons for rushing through our kids' routines are not based on some grand parenting plan but rather are due to our simply being in a hurry—and believing we are *suppose* to be in a hurry.

One of my favorite activities with my daughter is reading from a kid's Bible every night. No matter how late, no matter how tired, no matter anything, she will always say as she crawls into bed, "We need to read the Bible, Daddy." I'm smart enough to know children's stalling techniques and the art of drawing out bed times. But why on earth would I tell her that we don't have time to read a four-minute Bible story? Why would I teach her that her daddy doesn't have time to read the Bible to her and that maybe God doesn't have time for her either?

One morning last week my wife came upstairs (where I was hurriedly getting ready to leave) to tell me that my daughter was crying at the breakfast table. She had just been told that I wouldn't be home that night at bedtime. Through her fight to hold back a flood of tears, she said, "But Daddy didn't read the Bible to me the last two nights. This will be three nights in row!" I'm not sure where I "had to be" that morning. I don't remember where I "had to be" that night. I do remember her tears and that I came downstairs, Bible in hand, and read to her during breakfast.

I can't imagine saying, "I just don't have time," but I admit that I've done it. And I can't even tell you why.

Hurry sickness creates tension and anxiety and ultimately produces people who have no idea who they are or why they're here. Hurry sickness keeps us from enjoying life.

THE FATIGUE FACTOR

Author Lewis Grant coined the term "sunset fatigue" to describe the common condition of coming home at the end of a workday, after child shuffling, food-delivery ordering, or other hurry-up activities and just being too tired or too distracted or too wound up to care for those who need love and tenderness. Sunset fatigue causes the most important people in our lives to get our leftovers, since we've already given out our best to the red-zoned world.

Here, according to Grant, are the end-of-the-day behaviors that signal sunset fatigue:

You rush around at home even when there's no reason to.

You speak sharp words to your spouse and children, even when they've done nothing to deserve them.

You hurry your children along. You set up mock races ("Okay kids, let's see who can take a bath fastest"), which are really about your own need to complete the task.

You tell your family (and yourself) that everything will be okay "in just a week or two." It will always slow down "in just a week or two."

You indulge in self-destructive escapes: watching too much TV, abusing alcohol, or scanning pornographic websites.

You flop into bed with no sense of gratitude and wonder for the day; all you feel is fatigue.[7]

Jesus knew that the greatest and most serious consequence of hurry sickness was an ever-decreasing ability to love. He knew that we couldn't love Him or others while being in a hurry. Writing under the inspiration of God, the apostle Paul reminds us: "Love is patient" (1 Corinthians 13:4). Remember patience?

Jesus knew about fatigue, and He knew the value of slowing down. "Because so many people were coming and going that they did not even have a chance to eat, [Jesus] said to them [his disciples], 'Come with me by yourselves to a quiet place and get some rest'" (Mark 6:31). What will it take for you to slow down?

I ran into a man who had heard me speak and was trying to apply the advice I had given about slowing down. He related an incident in which he had let another person go before him in line at a store. Then he obeyed the traffic laws on the way to the bank. By slowing down enough to do kind and courteous and legal things on the way to the bank, he arrived at the bank a few minutes later than he otherwise would have. But, and here's the clincher, he avoided walking into the middle of a bank robbery. He was grateful to me for the message.

Yeah, and then I won the lottery. I don't blame you for being cynical. I'm not a big fan of people telling stories like this one. Like, what are the chances of being in bank robbery anyway—even for those of us who run red lights and cut people off in traffic?

Still, this man purposely slowed his daily pace and experienced a good outcome, and it got his attention. What will it take for you? A heart attack? An auto accident?

"Naw," you say. "It won't happen to me." Right.

Well, if not physical ailments or injury, what about relational ailments and injury? What about an empty heart? A meaningless life? What will it take for you to realize that a fast-paced, redlined life will always result in shallow relationships and a cold heart?

DYING IN THE RED ZONE

Most automobiles are equipped with an instrument known as a tachometer. The "tach" looks like the speedometer but is usually numbered from one to eight. These numbers measure how fast the engine is turning in rpm (revolutions per minute, in thousands).

Most tachometers have a red mark in the upper end of the numbers, indicating the "red zone." This can start anywhere from the five to the seven and will extend to the end of the gauge. Granted, most people who drive a car with an automatic transmission never look at the tachometer. Still, almost every car manual will declare—often in boxed and bold print—"Driving your car in the red zone will often cause irreparable damage to your engine." Because of this, many of today's newer cars come equipped with a computer that will prevent the engine from running at a harmful rpm level.

The warning is clear: if you run your engine at a higher pace than it was designed for, you will severely damage your motor.

If humans came with an operating manual, this warning would be printed in large, bold-faced type: "Constantly living your life in the red zone will cause irreparable damage to your heart, your soul, and your mind. It will also destroy your relationships." Sadly, we don't have a tachometer to give us a daily reading of how fast our life is running or a computer to shut us down.

But there are warning signs.

Heart disease, gastrointestinal disorders, and psychological maladies are on the increase. Poor diet and lack of exercise are part of the problem. Who has time to work out? But so are stress and the pace of life. Our bodies tell us to slow down, but instead we take a new pill, buy a new "sounds of nature" CD, or simply do nothing to address the problem. After all, in a few months we'll get a two-week vacation, which, when it comes, we can cram full of activity so we can forget how busy we are at work.

Besides the muffled cries of our bodies, many of us have the promptings from friends and family to cut the rpm. Occasionally we hear a sermon (maybe even an internal nudge from God?) on the psalmist's cry to "be still, and know that I am God" (Psalm 46:10). But many of us just keep on redlining. We can be quiet with God some other time.

Authentic, naked-soul relationships are never birthed and nurtured by running our lives harder, fuller, or faster. It doesn't work with God or with people. It just doesn't work at all.

WHY DO WE RUN TILL WE DROP?

You might argue that hurry sickness is not chosen; it's forced on us by the accelerated pace of life in general. After all, we can't all move to a monastery. If you believe your hurried and harried schedule is your only option, let me ask you one last, extremely important question: *Why* are you always in a hurry?

There are only three honest answers to choose from:

1. We are very poorly organized, or we're handicapped in the area of scheduling our time. We don't take the time to get organized, because

getting organized doesn't sound like a "productive" activity. So life is constantly complicated by things like, "Where are my shoes? Where's my watch? Where's my cell phone? Where's that other child we have?"

2. We are trying to do too much, so we cram our schedules too tight. We guarantee our own failure by failing to include a cushion in our schedule. I am the king of thinking, *I've got time to do just one more thing before I leave the office.* That "one more thing" often makes me rush. Instead, any sane person would realize we don't have to get one more thing done. We can leave the office on time. That one thing will still be there tomorrow.

3. We think we're supposed to hurry. Way too many of us think if we're not busy, hurried, multitasking, and always within seconds' reach of a cell phone, we're not fulfilling our purpose on this planet. We equate meaning with productivity. We're wrong.

You can look from one end of the Bible to the other and never find justification for pushing your days to the limit. The only scenarios I find where the Scriptures encourage someone to hurry are when they are fleeing for their life. We also find Isaiah chastising the people for telling God to hurry up and finish His work. On a normal, routine-life basis, God is telling us, "Be still before the LORD and wait patiently for him" (Psalm 37:7).

Being "in a hurry" is not something God values.

URGENT OR IMPORTANT?

Some simple phrases capture life so accurately and so succinctly that they stick in our mind. Such is the title of a classic booklet written by Charles Hummel, *The Tyranny of the Urgent!* Hummel wrote:

> Your greatest danger is letting the urgent things crowd out the
> important. The important task rarely must be done today, or

even this week. But the urgent tasks call for instant action. The momentary appeal of these tasks seems irresistible and important. But, in light of time's perspective their deceptive prominence fades; with a sense of loss we recall the important task pushed aside.[8]

At times, there are events in our life that are both important *and* urgent. Last fall my wife and I arrived at a junior high football game just after one of the players had been injured. I could only see half of the kid's jersey number, but I soon realized that the boy being carried off the field was my son Austin.

I went onto the field and saw that this was no routine injury. We needed to get Austin to the hospital. So the team's trainer and I carried this big offensive lineman, who was suffering unbearable pain, all the way to the parking lot. Getting my son to the hospital for the medical care he needed was both important and urgent.

But that's not a normal day. Most of what we encounter is either important or urgent, but not both. Most of what we consider to be urgent isn't the stuff that's most important. Urgent things revolve around getting dinner over with so we can hurry to a meeting. Or rushing the kids out the door so they won't miss the bus (which would cause us to lose more time by having to drive them to school). Or speeding to church so we can get a decent parking place and make a quick exit after the service. These things seem urgent, but they're not important.

The urgent things often keep us from experiencing the things that are truly important. The important things mandate that we s-l-o-w d-o-w-n. The habit of slowness, of not rushing, was Jesus's modus operandi. In Luke 8 we see Jesus being rushed by others to get to the bedside of Jairus's twelve-year-old daughter. The girl was dying, and yet Jesus stopped to help a woman who had been hemorrhaging for the same number of years that the little girl had been alive. I have to believe Jairus wanted to say, "Come on, Jesus, hurry it up! Get in the van. Let's go!" But Jesus never gave in to the tyranny of the urgent. Even in what we would all see as an urgent situation, He was not controlled by "needing" to hurry. He knew that God would always give Him enough time to get done what needed to be done.

What *Really* Needs to Get Done?

The day after my son was injured in a football game, I was scheduled to leave to speak at a weekend retreat two thousand miles from home. I won't go into the details of rearranged flights, postponed meetings, and abridged plans. But I will say that it is events like this that bring everything into perspective. For the next three months of wheelchairs, casts, crutches, and the accompanying family, school, and transportation issues, we were reminded on a daily basis just what is truly important. We spent more time together as a family. Siblings were serving other siblings (we took pictures). We had discussions about what God was teaching us through this event. We had kids and teenagers and adults sharing lessons of empathy with those families who live every day with a child who has a permanent disability.

We were reminded of what is important to us and what is important to God.

Brother Lawrence was a French monk who lived almost four hundred years ago. From his premonk life as a soldier to his years in a monastery, he sought to achieve inner peace through the realization that no matter what he was doing—eating, praying, washing pots and pans—God was with him. Brother Lawrence did not settle for knowing God's presence in theory or as an abstract truth. He sought to live it every moment. As such, he sought to constantly "practice the presence of God"; his desire was not to let a moment pass without acknowledging that God was with him.[9]

I realize many of you are practically shouting, "But he lived *four hundred years* ago! And the dude lived in a monastery, for crying out loud! What else did he have to do with his time?" But as Brother Lawrence knew (and as we also know, if we think about it), the tasks of anybody's day can and will distract us from God. He could certainly be in as much of a hurry scurrying to get meals prepared (and he didn't have all those great, time-saving gadgets) as you can be hurrying to get kids to soccer practice and ballet.

Acknowledging God's presence is something we have to practice, just as slowness has to be practiced. If we are ever to experience authentic, life-changing relationships, then we have to practice not hurrying, because the world has not decided that slowing down should be a priority. If you want to live the life God called you to, you must make that decision on your own.

So how do we cure hurry sickness? Here are some suggestions:

- Drive in the slow lane, and drive the speed limit. (I live in Indianapolis, home of the Indy 500, where people think the speed limit on Loop 465 is whatever you want it to be. But you can still drive the limit and not get run over.)
- Go through a day without taking your watch along.
- Let someone go ahead of you in a checkout line—and smile.
- Eat slowly (actually chew your food).
- Spend at least ten minutes at the beginning of your day sitting, reflecting, and praying for release from hurriedness.
- Seek solitude. In the midst (not instead of) your daily responsibilities, find times of quiet. Solitude is where we find comfort and freedom; it's where we escape hurry and rush. Solitude is the remedy

for busyness. Solitude is the beginning of the end of empty, meaningless relationships.

Slowing down means avoiding the noise and distraction of CD and MP3 players, cell phones constantly at our side, televisions and radios and DVD players and the Internet. Each of these will defeat the solitude that renews us. Seriously, you *cannot* take a phone call.

If you live in a state of constant noise and hurry, you will never have a meaningful relationship with your spouse or your kids. You will never have a meaningful relationship with your friends. And you will never have a meaningful relationship with God. Weariness and hurriedness prevent authentic relationships—always, every single time. Having a consistently tired and hurried body always results in soul fatigue, which always results in a decreased ability to love. Yes, always.

The Things That Don't Keep

When our third child was born, we were given a plaque by some dear grandparents. Personally, I am not big into knickknacks and cute sayings ("Hurry up and get in the van" is not cute). This plaque fell into that category; I thought it was cute but an unnecessary reminder. I thanked them for it, but then it found its place in the back of my daughter's closet.

The plague was simply a picture of a mother holding an infant. The caption read:

> Scrubbing and dusting can wait 'til tomorrow
> for children grow up, we have learned to our sorrow.
> So settle down cobwebs and dust go to sleep,
> I am rocking my baby and babies don't keep.

My "baby" is now in school full-time, loves to play with her girlfriends, and is *very* independent. My oldest is a teenager with football practice, skateboards, friends, and homework every day of the week. My middle son rocks on guitar, hangs with his buddies, and constantly works on one sport or another.

I don't have babies anymore; babies don't keep. Moments of simply holding them in my arms and rocking them to sleep don't keep. Moments of reading them bedtime stories don't keep. Moments of being "Daddy" instead of "Dad" don't keep.

And there's more. Moments with my wife don't keep. Moments simply to talk to my neighbors don't keep. Moments to reflect on my life, my God, my Savior, and my call in this world don't keep. Moments to change the world do not keep. Moments to live authentically in the lives of others do not keep.

You know what does keep? A lot! Mowing lawns will keep. So will cleaning the house, opening the mail, washing the car, and even reading the paper. No one at the end of his life will wish he had spent more time at the office. As your life winds down, who do you think will care if you had the best lawn in the neighborhood, your cars were always waxed, your house was always spotless, or even if you were salesperson of the month for forty-eight months running? Who will care, especially since those things that have caused so much hurry in your life will leave you with nobody who knows you well enough to truly care for you anyway? As your day winds down, who will care whether you finished your whole to-do list?

Your children will care. Your mate will care. The friends you could have will care. The friends you don't have will care.

Today I am home with my daughter, who is sick. As the day began, my wife and I decided she should stay home from school. I was able to work from home part of the day so she could go places she needed to go while the other two children were in school. It seemed like a good plan to me because I could get in a little writing while my daughter slept on the couch or watched videos.

That could have happened. Even when my daughter asked me to sit with her for "a while," it could have happened. Even when she asked me to play a board game with her, it could have happened. I could have said, "No, honey, Daddy has to get some work done. You just need to watch videos by yourself." That's what the "hurry up; you've got a deadline" person inside my head said.

But right now, my daughter won't keep.

Making Time

For many years Brother Lawrence was bothered by the thought that he wasn't an expert at prayer. He wrote, "Then one day I realized I would always be a failure at prayer; and I've gotten along much better ever since."[10] So often the frustration, anxiety, and worry that come from our failure to "get it all done" is due to believing the myth that it's actually possible to get it all done. Here's the truth: we will *never* get it all done. There will always be something else begging for our time and attention. We will always be a failure at getting it all done. Accept it.

But we do *not* have to be a failure at achieving authentic relationships. If there is one answer we will need to know on the "test of life" developed by our Creator, it is this: *you will never achieve deep, authentic relationships as along as you are living in the red zone.* And if there is one foolproof thing you can do to change that, it is to take the time to reflect honestly on life before you close your eyes at night. How about tonight?

Nearly everyone can recite some version of the fourth commandment: remember the Sabbath day and keep it holy (Exodus 20:8). We have all heard sermons, most of which we've ignored, on the importance of keeping a day for rest and reflection. But we need to remember something. At the end of *each day that God created something "good" for women and men,* the sovereign God of the universe stopped and observed all that He had done. And He reflected and said it was "good." At the end of the day, God reflected.

Do I end each day like that? Do you?

We can't stop to reflect on life without being changed. This is not a time to beat ourselves up for all we did wrong or for all we *didn't* get done. Instead, it's a process of reflecting on the important questions:

- Where did I fail to love others today as God wanted me to?
- When did I hurry unnecessarily?
- How can I slow down more tomorrow?
- Who in my life needs me to love them tomorrow?
- What are the wonderful gifts that God has filled my life with?

These questions will gradually help turn you into a more authentic lover of people.

I keep a sign on my desk that reads: "Do not sacrifice the glory of the eternal on the altar of the immediate." It's a reminder that the immediate gratification of my own desires often fails to serve the glory of a life lived for God and others. It reminds me to remain faithful to my wife in mind, body, and word. It reminds me that the things that don't scream for my time—prayer, reflection, family, friends—are the important things, and I must *make* time for them. It reminds me that the glory of a life lived for God is a life lived at a pace that allows time for people.

I'm called to love people, and people don't keep.

Reflection

The Big Idea

We live in a world that expects us to operate constantly in "hurry up" mode. Often, we rush because we're disorganized. Or we rush because we think we have to. We live disordered lives because we have disordered hearts. But we will *never* experience authentic love and naked-soul relationships if we refuse to slow down. God calls us to love, and love is not a microwaveable commodity.

Key Verse

"Because so many people were coming and going that they did not even have a chance to eat, he said to them, 'Come with me by yourselves to a quiet place and get some rest.'" (Mark 6:31)

Answering Questions

- Are you in a hurry? Do you know why?
- Do you see the necessity of slowing down? If not, are you willing to take the pace of your life before God in prayer and wait to see what He says?
- Are you ready to get out of the red zone? There are times we must hurry, when something is both important and urgent. But what truly characterizes your life? If you want to change the world through loving God and people, you must eliminate hurry sickness from your life.

Prayer

Sovereign God, You are the Lord of all time: yesterday, today, and forever. Thank You that I have the example of Jesus, who never gave in to hurry but always put time for prayer, time for You, and time for people at the top of His list. May I learn from His example. May I have the courage and strength to s-l-o-w d-o-w-n. Change my heart, Lord, from disordered to peaceful. Be in my mind this day and every day as You teach me the importance of simply being still. Amen.

Six

Unplug the Microwave Life

The Relational Damage of Impatience and Anger

There are two main human sins from which
all the others derive: Impatience and indolence.

—FRANZ KAFKA

Amy and I bought two big-ticket items with the money we received on our wedding day: a bed and a microwave oven. What else do newlyweds need? A nice new bed so we'd have something on which to put all those sheets and bedspreads we received as wedding gifts and to do what all newlyweds do (see my first book). And a microwave oven to make life easier for a couple of DINKs (dual income, no kids—even though the two incomes were of a youth minister and a schoolteacher).

Back then, you couldn't just walk into Wal-Mart and buy a microwave for $39.95. Our first one cost more than $400.00. I'm not kidding. It had no bells or whistles, but inherent in that machine was the promise of great new experiences, like reheating coffee in the mug, cooking vegetables quickly, and being able to participate in one of the greatest inventions of the eighties (even better than Cabbage Patch Kids and Sony Walkmans): microwave popcorn.

No longer did we have to get out the big skillet and the oil and the oversized lid and spend as much as fifteen minutes popping corn. Instead, we could microwave it in less than three minutes. Wow.

The convenience and efficiency are addictive. The first appliance that all three of my kids learned to use, even before their electric toothbrushes, was the microwave. It was definitely before they learned to use the vacuum. We're still working on that one. Microwaving is great, but there's a downside. Microwaves have taught us that we can make almost anything fast, so now we want to microwave life itself. We want all the benefits of "instant" wisdom, love, relationships, and spiritual and emotional maturity. But life doesn't work that way.

As I mentioned in the last chapter, trend watchers in the 1960s predicted that, with all the new timesaving devices, life in the future would be crammed with leisure. In truth, timesaving devices have produced little more than a really impatient society. Normal life just seems to take too long. And it fuels our anger and impatience.

MICROWAVE FAILURE

When I was working in senior high youth ministry, it wasn't unusual for well-meaning parents to contact me and quietly share the struggles they were having with their teenager. Sometimes they were seeking advice and counsel. But often they simply asked me to spend some time with their kids to try to help them through a tough time. Their hope was that I'd hang with the kids and get them interested in the things of God. I always welcomed such an opportunity.

Every so often, however, there would be a parent whose adolescent was having *major* problems, getting into all sorts of trouble. In some cases, further probing would uncover a series of poor parenting choices. I'd find out there were no set boundaries for the teen, there was a lack of warmth from the parents, or the parents were so involved in other things that their presence was barely felt at home. The rebellious, troublesome kid was a result. It was not unusual for the dad or mom to say, "Can you get him to a Christian camp or something that will get him out of this quickly?"

I wanted to say, "You've had fifteen years to screw this poor kid up, so don't count on six days in the mountains to produce a mature, selfless, problem-free kid."

There is no such thing as good microwave parenting. Socrates wondered how people "who were so careful in the training of a colt could be so indifferent in the training of their children."[1] Not much has changed in two thousand years.

In my work as a professional counselor, couples often come for help after spending years demolishing each other's hearts. They have suffered for so long, and now their pain cries out for immediate relief. Research shows that most people who seek marriage counseling do so *six years* after one of them concludes they have a serious problem. If you break your leg and wait six years to go the doctor, you're going to have much greater problems than the initial fractured fibula. Still, no matter how long they have neglected their relationship, couples in distress want help; they want the pain to go away, and they want it to happen *yesterday!*

But you can't microwave selflessness or intimacy in marriage. And you can't microwave the one thing each of us wants the most: authentic relationships.

MICROWAVE ANGER

Our insatiable desire for more speed, from quick cooking to fast weight loss to a speedier Internet connection, has another consequence that we don't often recognize. Speed feeds our anger, which grows out of control when things don't happen as quickly as we want. Just think about road rage, violence in the workplace, and the general breakdown of civility in our society. It seems that common courtesy just takes too long.

The problem is not speed, or even anger itself; it's anger that is *uncontrolled*. Anger is a natural response when our body (or the bodies of those we care about) is threatened. As such, anger is a self-defense mechanism. When Jesus overturned the tables of the moneychangers and cleared the temple of those who were selling animals for ritual sacrifice, He was defending His Father's house (Matthew 21:12–13). Anger is both an emotion and a physiological reaction. When we react to a threat with the "fight, freeze, or flight" syndrome, adrenaline rushes to the bloodstream, our heart rate increases, our blood pressure rises, our muscles receive a blast of energy, and even our eyes dilate for better peripheral vision. We can't control the arrival of the response. But we can control what we do with it. We don't have to allow anger to grow out of control.

Two days ago my eleven- and thirteen-year-old sons had a disagreement that included some yelling and shoving. When we were discussing the situation afterward, my thirteen-year-old kept saying, "But he made me so angry." I kept stopping him and saying, "No. You may not have liked what your brother did, but your anger is *yours*, not his. What you do with it is your responsibility."

The words "you make me so angry" form one of the most frequently used phrases in the English language, and it's one of the most wrongly used phrases there is. Our anger is *ours,* not theirs. It's a tough concept to accept, but we must accept it, because it's true.

If we didn't have the ability to control our responses, Paul would not have written: "'In your anger do not sin': Do not let the sun go down while you are still angry" (Ephesians 4:26). He does not say that we should never be angry. But self-centered and uncontrolled anger is not simply a physiological response. It's sin. Sinful anger prevents us from being close to people and steals the greatest desire of our hearts (see James 1:20).

We are an angry society. Movies and even cartoons praise angry victims who become vigilantes, while newspapers carry headlines of the death and devastation of innocent people resulting from anger—often one spouse against another or even a parent against his or her children. And apart from the potential for violence, unmanaged anger leaves us lonely, afraid, and without meaning. A person who lives in a state of anger will never contribute to positive change or experience true intimacy with others.

Gene was one of the angriest men I'd ever encountered. When he came to my counseling office, he didn't get loud, and he never threatened me or anyone else. He was proud of the fact that he didn't "lose it" very often. But his body language, his choice of words, and especially his eyes warned of an active volcano. The magma was churning just below the surface.

Gene came to see me because he wanted to know how to keep his wife from leaving him. He admitted there had been problems over the years, but they had always hung in there. Now Gene wanted me to convince his wife that she needed to stay in their marriage. But he didn't want to admit that his chronic anger, which had made his wife a victim of emotional abuse, was the thing that was pushing her away. He didn't want to admit that his anger had worked so well at keeping his wife at a distance—far enough away that she couldn't "hurt him"—that now it was easy for her to leave.

Newton Hightower, director of the Center for Anger Resolution, says, "Destructive anger hurts your health, makes you miserable, blocks solutions, wastes your energy, keeps you helpless, invites attacks, imprisons your spirit, wrecks human relations, gives you headaches, causes accidents, ruins restful sleep and turns a love life into a lonely life."[2] Anger destroys everything God designed real relationships to provide. Said another way, anger creates a world that is the exact opposite of what your heart so deeply desires.

We long for authentic, heart-soothing relationships; we desperately long for an end to our loneliness. But here's the catch. Without love, we feel disconnected and without purpose—and that makes us angry. But the simmering anger that is caused by our disconnection prevents us from drawing close to others. It is a vicious cycle. The way we act prevents us from laying hold of our deepest desires, which fuels more of the behavior that keeps us from engaging in authentic relationships.

Gene's story has a sad ending. He lost his wife, his children, and even his job. He was lonely when he was married, and he was even more lonely after his marriage ended. Gene left therapy years ago, and if he has not dealt with his anger, I know one thing for sure. He's still lonely.

GETTING ON TOP OF ANGER

Hurry sickness causes people to rush at a breakneck pace from sunup to sundown. If you haven't dealt with your compulsion to cram more and more into your days and nights, then you'll never overcome your anger. And you will never be able to get on top of your impatience. Hurried people are frequently angry people—even ragingly angry people. Hurried people are by nature impatient. Hurried people don't have time to meet the commitments they already have, which means they certainly don't have time to pursue naked-soul relationships. Hurried people are often angry, impatient, and lonely people.

Look at the driver who gets impatient in traffic. You have an angry person who is hurried, and he believes the drivers in front of him have singled him out to be delayed. He grips the steering wheel and fumes at a 1995 Chevy or a 2002 Toyota. It's more acceptable to vent at "things" than it is at people. When we don't have a relationship with other people—they're just anonymous drivers in slow-moving vehicles—we feel more justified in our emotional eruptions. The raging motorist hardly recognizes that other drivers are people—real, breathing, soul-possessing, made-in-the-image-of-God people—all of them sitting in traffic and all of them being delayed, just as he is. Anger blinds us to our need for love—and others' need for love too.

You will make significant progress toward controlling your anger and deepening your love for people if you begin to allow slowness to invade your day. If you start practicing slowness on a regular basis, and if you add the practice of daily reflection to your routine, you will become aware of places and, more important, people in your day where you display edginess and irritation. You'll become aware of others and more aware of your need to change.

You need to know (and probably have discovered already) that simply "willing" a complete change in your life won't bring about immediate, permanent results. But it *is* a great first step.

When I was in high school, a group of Young Life leaders bought me my first study Bible. Inside the front cover was a handwritten note: "Tim, 'For I am confident of this very thing, that He who began a good work in you will perfect it until the day of Christ Jesus,' Phil. 1:6 [NASB]." I didn't have a clue what that meant. I was a sixteen-year-old very deep into "the world revolves around me." I didn't even know that "Phil. 1:6" meant it was part of the Bible. But what the college-age volunteer leaders knew was this: I had made a decision to accept Christ and follow God, and therefore God's transforming work in me had begun.

The Message version of that Philippians verse says it this way: "There has never been the slightest doubt in my mind that the God who started this great work in you would keep at it and bring it to a flourishing finish on the very day Christ Jesus appears."

God will transform us. But we don't serve a microwave God. His work always takes time. Complete transformation will not be completed in this life, but it will begin if we spend the needed time with God—the needed calm and quiet time with God. But swimming in a sea of anger and impatience will thwart that transformation.

In Romans, Paul writes, "And do not be conformed to this world, but be transformed by the renewing of your mind, so that you may prove what the will of God is, that which is good and acceptable and perfect" (Romans 12:2, NASB). The word *transformed* in Greek is *metamorpho*, from which we get our word *metamorphosis. Meta* in this case means "form," and *morph* means "to change." At the end of a metamorphosis, we have changed form. We've made a complete alteration. But it takes time and patience. And it takes our getting a handle on our anger.

These same things are required to change our relationships with people.

DO THE HARD THINGS

Many people who recognize their hunger for authentic relationships want to enjoy such relationships, but they also want to reduce the energy and inconvenience that it takes to develop them. We acknowledge that we'd love to be remembered not as a person who worked hard and made a lot of money, but as someone who cared for others and whose love and selflessness made life better for others. Will you make the time for that to happen?

If we don't learn the discipline of slowness, we'll never achieve those goals. Tara is a twenty-something friend of mine, and this is how she describes life:

> I think instant gratification is definitely what we as young adults
> want. Look at our society in general. We hate sitting in traffic
> jams or waiting in line at the grocery store and even in fast food
> places. If you have to wait for more than a minute you begin to
> complain!
>
> Trying to lose weight is [a] perfect [example]. I work out all
> the time and try to diet but I want to see results *now,* not five
> months from now. So then you begin looking into the fastest
> way to lose the weight, whether that be popping pills, not eating,
> or a certain diet. Our generation was brought up on the fast
> foods of the world where we don't wait for anything!

Once again, the microwave life gets in the way. Many of our heart's deepest desires are thwarted by our mind's choices. And many of those choices get made without our realizing that there is a disconnect between what we want and what we do. To experience true change, we must realize where this disconnect is occurring in our lives.

In a survey conducted for the Massachusetts Mutual Life Insurance Corporation, parents stated that the greatest threat to the family was parents' inability to spend enough time with their children. Thirty-five percent of respondents believed that time constraints were the number-one reason associated with the decline of family values. Additionally, 63 percent of participants stated that their family is their greatest source of pleasure; they just wish they had more time to spend together. And yet, in spite of their expressed wish for more time, an amazing two-thirds of those surveyed said they would most likely take a job that required more time away from home if it offered higher income or greater prestige.[3] How can that be?

At first glance, people may say that it's because we value money over people—even the people we love the most. That may be true in part. But I'm convinced that the bigger answer is that we believe having extra money and more prestige will somehow produce more closeness in family relationships. We think we can show love to our families by providing them with a lot of stuff. The other reason, whether we know it or not, is that it's just safer to work longer hours to make more money so we can give more stuff to our families. As in most areas of life, we don't change because we are frightened by the unknown. We don't pour ourselves into people because deep relationships are unknown and uncertain. I might share something very personal, and the other person might reject me or even judge me. That's just too big a risk, so I keep everyone else at arm's length.

I'd never tell you that naked-soul relationships are not a huge risk. People and relationships don't come with a guarantee. You might take the initiative to befriend someone, and the person might not respond in the way you had hoped. People may accept and welcome an expression of care and love, or they may turn their back on you. That's the risk.

The infamous television character Archie Bunker was asked, "Why are relationships so hard?" He replied, "Because people are in them, and people are screwups."[4] He's right, but screwups—ours and those of others—can be overcome with patience and love. Authentic relationships aren't safe or convenient, but they are the only antidote to loneliness.

SICK AND TIRED OF BEING SICK AND TIRED?

If you're ready for real change, it's time to take some big risks. If you find yourself impatient and angry, you need to first decide that you're willing to exchange the pain of your anger for the initial uncertainty and discomfort of letting go of your anger.

Ready? First, make the time (you have to make it; you'll never find it) to be by yourself. Quietly. Get up earlier, stay up later, turn off the television, leave the house if you need to. (But do this without giving up more sleep, since a lack of sleep is another contributor to anger.) The time of day and location don't matter as much as doing what you have to do to get time alone. Co-op a deal with your spouse where one of you stays home with the kids and the other heads for the late-night coffee shop. Tomorrow night, switch roles. And take a journal, a Bible, and this book with you.

Then, with the time protected, s-l-o-w-l-y read and think through the verses of Scripture that follow and those that end this chapter. Pause after each one and reflect on what it means. Write it out in your journal in your own words. (I've interspersed different versions of Scripture, and if you are able, I encourage you to do the same thing with the verses that you look up. Go to the library and check out different Bible versions.) Get alone, get quiet, shut out distractions. Stop, reflect, write. Pray for God to meet you and teach you, and then begin.

Find a verse (or a few verses) from below or in the list at the end of this chapter that speaks most directly to what you are feeling. What is God putting His finger on in your life? What does He want you to confront?

Concentrate on that verse or verses. Read them slowly, and read them again slowly. Read them several times through, praying as you read. What people come to mind? What situations does God bring to mind? What emotions are you feeling? Identify the people, situations, and feelings. Write them down in your journal.

Now read what you have written and pray over it. Ask God to open your spirit to His work in the areas of impatience, anger, relationships, loneliness, and authenticity. Tell God about your need, your desires, and your struggles. Ask Him to address those areas of your life that prevent you from taking the risk of authentic relationships. Tell Him that you are ready to let go of anger and impatience.

Again, I am listing a few verses here; there is a longer list at the end of the chapter. Read, reflect, record…and pray.

A patient man has great understanding,
     but a quick-tempered man displays folly.
          (Proverbs 14:29)

Do not be quick in spirit to be angry or vexed, for anger
and vexation lodge in the bosom of fools.
(Ecclesiastes 7:9, AMP)

Be joyful in hope, patient in affliction, faithful in prayer.
(Romans 12:12)

Slowness to anger makes for deep understanding;
     a quick-tempered person stockpiles stupidity.
          (Proverbs 14:29, MSG)

Love is patient, love is kind. It does not envy, it does not boast, it
is not proud. (1 Corinthians 13:4)

He who is slow to anger is better than the mighty,

And he who rules his spirit, than he who captures a city.

(Proverbs 16:32, NASB)

Quiet down before GOD,

be prayerful before him. (Psalm 37:7, MSG)

After reading, reflecting, and writing in your journal what God brought to mind through a verse or verses, answer these questions: What does your Creator think about the necessity of patience? What is His view of a person with uncontrolled anger? Go ahead; write down the answers.

The goal is neither guilt nor perfection. And that is something I thank God for every day. Even in the middle of writing this chapter, I lost my cool with a hotel clerk. And get this, I was in town to fulfill a speaking engagement. At a *Christian conference!* Oh sure, I can try to blame it on being tired (we arrived at 3:00 a.m.), the fact that this was the third trip in a row where this particular hotel made a reservation error, yada-yada-yada. The fact is, I did not show the patience, grace, and control of anger that I should have.

And let's not even begin the conversation about how we shouldn't let ourselves be taken advantage of. I agree. But I can stand for what's right and still display patience and kindness. And I can say I'm sorry when I mess up.

The questions related to whether we are controlling our anger are these:

1. Am I allowing God to begin the process of transforming me?

2. Am I making progress in my quest to become more Christlike?

Are you sick and tired of being sick and tired of your anger, impatience, and loneliness? Do you believe that God is sick and tired of it too? It's time to give in and let Him begin changing you.

NO QUICK FIX

We recently repainted a large portion of the inside of our home. Knowing it was going to be a big project, I invested in an electric paint roller. The test area for trying out this new timesaver was my middle son's room. Two coats of paint went on smoothly and looked good. And it was fast! Like most guys, at the end of the second coat I rounded up the family so they could tell me how great it looked. Then I went downstairs to take care of a few things and returned about thirty minutes later to clean up the wonderful painting machine.

I grabbed the whole shebang—paint can, base, paint hose, and roller—and headed to the laundry room, where the sink was. In spite of the fact that cleanup took twice as long as normal compared to washing out a paint brush and low-tech roller, I was still way ahead of the game. Then I left the laundry room to head back upstairs to finish cleaning up the odds and ends.

That's when I noticed a trail of paint across the tile floor. I guess I'd dripped a little. Knowing that acrylic paint would clean up easily off the tile, I headed down the hall and through the kitchen to get water and a rag. That's when I noticed another paint trail. There was a moment of relief when I saw the trail stop five feet from the stairs—where the carpet started. Whew! Then I rounded the banister. The paint trail on the carpeted stairway was thicker and more pronounced, with dark paint winding all the way upstairs. I followed it down the upstairs hall only to find even bigger pools of paint on the floor of my son's room.

Angry? What do you think? Frustrated with myself? Most of all. During the time I had been showing off my work and then kibitzing downstairs, gravity had brought a large amount of paint through the paint tube and into the roller cover of my timesaving power roller. I hadn't seen it, so

I'd dribbled the trail all the way downstairs. My timesaving wonder now kept me up till two in the morning with brushes, rags, and supermega spot remover.

I know, I know. The first response of many of you is a well-deserved "You goofball!" But all I could think of during those hours of scrubbing carpets and floors was how much time this new timesaving device was costing me.

You've experienced something like that too, haven't you? Be it by purchasing the latest planner or PDA, buying into the latest fad diet, trying to master a new financial wizard software, or any of a thousand other things, you've been there. We want improvements to happen, and we want them to happen fast!

This *never* works with people. It also never works when trying to develop patience or when trying to manage your anger. Trying to make these needed changes fast will either postpone the result or ultimately prevent it altogether. Some of you want to read the verses without journaling or pray without reading or do it all in three minutes while shoving down toast at breakfast. That will *never* work. You have to choose to invest a lot of time. Are you ready to do that?

THE *A* WORD

We need one more thing to help achieve this goal of change. *Accountability.* And that scares us almost as much as taking the risk of immersing ourselves in authentic relationships.

Adam and Eve didn't want to be held accountable. After they disobeyed God, Adam said, "It was the woman you gave me..." Eve said, "It was the serpent..." No personal responsibility. No willingness to be held accountable for their choices and actions.

Neither you nor I will succeed in dealing with our anger or our impatience if we expect it to happen either in a microwave or in a vacuum. It doesn't happen quickly, and it doesn't happen in isolation. We need others to help us to change, to encourage us, and to challenge us when we mess up. We all need accountability.

YOU STILL HAVE TIME

If you got alone, got quiet, and took your time in reading and reflecting on the verses of Scripture, then you should be feeling less of a desire to beat yourself up for the times you've failed. Instead, you should be feeling more of a longing to experience the kind of life God calls you to. The question now is, what are you going to do about it?

There is a story that comes out of the Spanish civil war concerning a captain and his men as they huddled in a dark, damp cellar, silently waiting for the dawn. Just before sunrise they were to lead an assault on a nearby city. The captain and his men tried to sleep, but they could only doze fitfully throughout the night. Early in the morning the young officer felt someone touch his shoulder. He jumped up, gun in hand, ready to go into battle—and perhaps even to die.

It was a fellow officer who had awakened him to announce that the attack had been called off. The weary captain slumped back onto the floor with a dazed look of relief on his tired face. The other officer realized what must be going through his mind and said, "Captain, you've been given more time, haven't you? What are you going to do with it?"[5]

There are, on occasion, events that occur in life that cause us to stop and take stock of the limited commodity of *time*. You may have heard the story of Alfred Nobel, the inventor of dynamite. When he realized the destructive power of what he had created and the lives that would be lost, he took much of the enormous fortune that he had amassed and used it to fund what you and I know as the Nobel Prize. But you might not know what caused his realization. It was an inaccurate newspaper headline that read: Alfred Nobel, Dynamite King, Dies. The obituary that followed let Nobel know that if his life remained on its present course and things went unchanged, his name throughout history would be synonymous with the king of destruction.[6] He was Scrooge being confronted by the Ghost of Christmas Yet To Come.

Few of us experience such an event that convinces us it's time for a significant change. But each of us has the freedom to choose that, starting today, we're going to make a change.

Are you going to deal with your lack of patience? If the answer is yes, then I suggest you take the journal where you have recorded your thoughts and Scripture paraphrases and sit quietly *at least five out of the next seven mornings* and read—slowly and reflectively—every word you have written. Then read it again, this time in the form of a personalized prayer. If you want the blessings of patience and if you want a life of authenticity with others, you must reflect on God's Word and apply it to your life on a daily basis.

And what about your anger? If you want to deal with your anger, solemnly determine that things *must* change. If you're still not sure, ask the people you work with and live with if they've been burned by your anger. Make sure they know you really want an honest answer. (If they're frightened by your anger, then how likely are they to tell you the truth?) Promise them that you will not get angry over an honest response.

You must take responsibility for your anger. Don't use the excuse that others make you mad. Anger is a response, but you choose to control it or not. Others might do things you dislike. They may even do things to intentionally hurt you. But the anger is yours. Each of us chooses how we will react.

Our anger keeps people at arm's length or beyond. If we want to know and be known, if we want to love and be loved, we must realize that anger will short-circuit that process every time. It will prevent us from ever experiencing God's amazing, everyday solution to loneliness.

If you want to change, you must do these things. Do not short-circuit what I've laid out and then complain that nothing has changed. There are no shortcuts. You must choose to work and work hard.

Do you want an end to your loneliness? Then you must be patient. You must be calm and in control of your anger. You must choose to do things differently.

As of this moment, you and I have been given more time. What are we going to do with it?

Verses for Journaling and Prayer

2 Peter 3:9

Ecclesiastes 7:9

1 Thessalonians 5:14

James 5:7–8

Psalm 103:8

Proverbs 29:11

Jonah 4:2

Mark 3:5

Ephesians 4:31

Colossians 3:8

Psalm 4:4

Reflection

The Big Idea

It's impossible to microwave love and authentic relationships. People take time. It's also impossible to have a life full of love if we have a heart full of anger. Love is patient and kind, calm and controlled. God calls us, with the time we have left, to make the changes we need in the areas of patience and anger.

Key Verse

"Post this at all the intersections, dear friends: Lead with your ears, follow up with your tongue, and let anger straggle along in the rear. God's righteousness doesn't grow from human anger." (James 1:19–20, MSG)

Answering Questions

- Are you ready to unplug the microwave and deal with your anger? If so, you must make the time to carry out the exercises described in this chapter, reflecting and journaling on the verses listed.
- Are you willing to be in this for the long haul? Neither impatience nor anger can be dealt with quickly. Find an accountability partner and start the journey now.
- Are you ready to become a patient, loving, caring person? Great. Because that is what God wants too. Let's both, in prayer, get to work.

Prayer

Loving Father, You are so patient and kind with me, waiting for me to finally "get it" and realize that the pace, impatience, and fury of this world are not the life You call me to live. Gracious God, speak to me. May Your Word be ever present in my mind as I seek to live a life that serves as an example of Your patience, Your kindness, Your peace, and Your love. May my life reflect Your authentic love. Amen.

Seven

Sex and the Idiot Box

Why It's Easier to Be Lonely Than to Be Loved

I find television very educating.
Every time somebody turns on the set,
I go into the other room and read a book.
—GROUCHO MARX

The remarkable thing about television is that
it permits several million people to laugh at the same joke
and still feel lonely.
—T. S. ELIOT

It was an unusual sight, to be sure. I was in graduate school and had gone to a classmate's condo to work on a project. Around 10:00 p.m. we heard someone (or something) knocking around on the front porch. My friend wasn't expecting visitors, and since it was late, I told her I'd go see who—or what—it was. As I approached the door, instead of hearing sounds from all over the porch, I heard just four raps. Right on the other side of the door.

I couldn't see anything through the peephole, so I walked to the window and peered out. I said to my friend, "You have *got* to come see this."

On the porch was a huge, dazed, bewildered skunk with a glass jar stuck on his head. To be specific, it was a Miracle Whip jar, and the poor animal was banging into everything in sight. A skunk was not too unusual for the Texas hill country, but with a jar on its head? That *was* different.

I've had pets ranging from horses and dogs to squirrels and rabbits. But I'd never had the urge to befriend a skunk. Still, concerned about what may or may not happen to this particular skunk—and urged on by my friend— I ventured outside, ready to make a headlong dive over the railing and into the bushes if needed.

The skunk, meanwhile, wandered over, stopped at my feet, and looked up at me through the bottom of the jar, as if to say, "Hey, buddy, can you give me a hand here?" Thus began the rescue process. I attempted unsuccessfully to pull the jar off the animal's head. Smashing the jar with a hammer came to mind, but that approach, though fun, would increase my chances of getting sprayed to about 137 percent. So I asked my friend to bring me a pair of pliers. For the next few minutes I slowly broke off the narrow rim of the unusual headwear, allowing the jar to finally slip off the head of my trusting animal acquaintance. At the moment of freedom, I remained ready to take my chances with the six-foot drop over the railing.

But I didn't need to leap. The skunk never did the ground-pounding, tail-raising dance that skunks do when they feel threatened. He simply looked at me and then turned slowly and walked off. Honestly, all I could think of was the Kraft Foods ad campaign for Miracle Whip, which showed distressed consumers scraping the jar to get every last bit of salad dressing for their sandwich. If only I'd had a video camera.

Reflecting today on the skunk with a jar mask, I realize that he was a great example of being blind to the thing that has you trapped. A transparent cage is still a cage.

BREAK THE JAR

At some point we all have had our heads stuck in a jar. We're staggering around, banging into things, wondering what it is that has us trapped. And after the invisible cage creates enough disruption in our lives, we begin to hope for a solution.

When we think of addicts and addictions, images of nicotine fiends, drug abusers, and alcoholics usually come to mind. And while all of those war against real relationships, such addictions are not the invisible cages I'm referring to. Most people, even those in alcoholic denial, can see the cage of drugs or nicotine and recognize the bars that trap them.

I'm talking about a different type of cage—one we don't see. For instance, many of us sense the relational void in our lives. But we seek to minimize the pain of loneliness through destructive coping mechanisms, such as getting too much sleep or engaging in too much work or obsessively pursuing exercise, dieting, eating, or body shaping. A more obvious but still invisible cage is casual sex. People believe that casual sex and trial relationships create a sort of starter intimacy, a warmup for the real thing. We think we're practicing for lasting intimacy down the road, not realizing we're trapped in a cage.

Or we give in to the lure of television. Americans spend incredible amounts of money on high-resolution televisions with surround sound and digital cable or satellite reception. It's just a way to relax and refresh ourselves, so we'll be better equipped to deal with the real world of real relationships. Right? Wrong. For many, television is an invisible cage that traps our time and attention while shutting out real relationships.

We devote ourselves to things like sex and the idiot box because we wrongly believe they will provide a respite from our loneliness. We don't realize that each of these is an invisible prison that not only keeps us from getting out, but also keeps others from getting in.

Selling Sex

Anytime you see the words *real* and *sex* together, be forewarned—someone is trying to sell you something. The same is true when sex is attached to the words *new, secret, breakthrough,* or *revolutionary.* Every time you stand in the grocery store checkout line you're bombarded with magazine headlines promising the latest insights, methods, positions, and secrets to lead you to the ultimate sexual experience.

But if magazines and tabloids have the answer to life-fulfilling sex, why do they come back month after month promising the same thing all over again? Aren't the ten secrets to the sex of your wildest dreams enough? Why would you need the next installment—a guaranteed method for Fourth of July sex *every time!*—again next month?

Why? Because even if you could follow all of this advice, and even if you practiced every single technique until you mastered it, you would still gain only an incremental boost in sexual satisfaction. And then you'd find that the longer you practice the same technique in search of sexual perfection, the less appeal it will hold. It just won't be that satisfying after a while, so you'll need another *new* discovery next month.

We're like a hamster on an exercise wheel, working harder but never making any lasting progress. We need to get off the wheel that tells us that mastering the pleasures of sex will satisfy the longings in our hearts. Sex is about pleasure, to be sure. *But pleasure is not primary.* And neither is procreation.

In my book *Sacred Sex,* I shared the story of Kevin and Brenda. They were each other's "first and only" when it came to sexual intercourse. Now, fifteen years, two kids, and numerous sexual experiments later, they were in my counseling office hoping to learn something new so they could regain the "spark" they had lost. Actually, this was a repeat of the complaint they'd had two years earlier.

Brenda and Kevin had swallowed the lie that great sex is about positions, frequency, variety, and orgasm. As far as they were concerned, the point of sex was pleasure. I had worked with them two years earlier to reframe their understanding of sex. According to God's design, the purpose of sex is not orgasm but oneness.

When we had finished our first few counseling sessions, Brenda and Kevin at first enjoyed the fruits of focusing on oneness rather than orgasm. They learned that sexual intimacy is part of the bigger picture of spiritual and relational intimacy in marriage: making time for one another, sharing their hearts with each other, praying together, making each other a top priority. In that context, sex became an important component of the bigger process of drawing closer—the two becoming one in marriage. They still fully enjoyed the sensations of sexual union, of course, but now sex had a deeper meaning. It benefited their entire relationship, not just their need for sexual release.

But before long they gave in to hurry sickness and expected microwave results from their sex life. Within a few months, they fell back into their former pattern of allowing other things to crowd out time devoted to their relationship. And predictably, their sex life suffered. But instead of working to build up their nonsexual intimacy, Kevin concluded that they needed something new to spice up their love life. Specifically, he felt that Brenda's breasts were too small. At his urging, she agreed to breast augmentation.

For a while, the novelty of this change, combined with the need for new lingerie, produced a higher level of sexual passion. And for a while, Kevin was more attentive to his wife outside the bedroom. But after a few months this, too, failed to bring permanent change; the spark was gone again, and they wondered what had put it out. When they returned to my counseling office, they were right back where they had started.[1]

Know this truth: the "Big O" of sex is not orgasm; it's oneness. Aiming for pleasure is like trying to hit a constantly moving target. When we pursue pleasure as the highest and best goal of sex, it will always fail to satisfy, because sex is subject to the law of diminishing returns: something that delivers a certain level of pleasure today will fail to provide that same level of pleasure tomorrow. So to sustain the same pleasure experience, we have to "up" the stimulation. This is the same reason a drug addict moves from a less potent drug to a harder one. It's why films and video games must increase their levels of gore and violence. It's why holding hands is a thrill for a while, but the excitement wears off, and so we move on to kissing and then to petting and then to sex. But when we reach the end, what do you do to deliver the increasing level of pleasure you're seeking?

A huge part of our God-given yearning to connect soul to soul with another person is an innate desire to become one sexually. Yet this desire will never find full satisfaction outside the God-designed safeguards of entering into the commitment and covenant of marriage and approaching sex as the route to oneness, rather than orgasm. When we remove those safeguards, having sex is like taking the hard drive out of a computer, laying it on a table, and expecting the hard drive to accomplish the role is was created for. By itself, it won't do you any good.[2] Likewise, you can't disconnect sex from the one thing that makes it work and then just keep trying new techniques, expecting that with all the extra effort you'll somehow force sex to supply you with major fulfillment. It won't.

If you set sexual pleasure as your goal, then sex will lead to nothing but frustration in one of three ways. One, it will continually fail to satisfy, and you'll end up either avoiding sex or growing apathetic toward it. Or two, sex will simply be tolerated, seen as a necessary evil or a duty that you perform for someone else's satisfaction. One person receives pleasure; the other person is saddled with an obligation. Or three, sex will provide you with yet another hamster wheel. You'll be running and running, seeking a greater thrill, letting lust run amuck, delving into pornography, affairs, and every other kind of sexual deviance. You'll be working harder than ever at achieving sexual pleasure, trying everything that's available, and still not finding what your heart desires. You've met someone, haven't you, who gets all the sex that anyone could want, yet is still empty and very lonely?

Sex is a great and glorious gift from God. He created it to bring immeasurable joy and deep personal connection with another human. As a matter of fact, it is intended to create the *deepest* personal connection possible between two of God's children. It is a celebration of oneness that plays a vital role in eradicating loneliness.

But sex will *never* bring ultimate fulfillment and lasting connection outside the covenant of marriage and the knowledge of its God-given purpose for oneness. It will never provide an intimate connection with a spouse if our goal is pleasure by way of quantity and variety. That's why a lot of people who are having a lot of sex still find themselves, imagine this, extremely lonely.

NEEDING WATER, CRAVING SALT

And then there's the problem of pornography. Someone has said that a person seeking sexual satisfaction through pornography is like a man dying of thirst yet craving salt. We consume more and more of what we believe will bring an end to our yearning, and we find that it only intensifies our desire for more. Addictions of all sorts could be described in that way. Another apt description is captured in the title of a book by Professor Edward Welch, *Addictions: A Banquet in the Grave.* The idea is taken from Proverbs 9, which describes what it's like to fall for the enticing words of a seductress:

> "Stolen water is sweet;
>> food eaten in secret is delicious!"
> But little do they know that the dead are there,
>> that her guests are in the depths of the grave.
>> (Proverbs 9:17–18)

We think we're finding satisfaction for the longings of our heart and soul. We don't realize that we're enjoying a meal that will ultimately destroy us. We long for love, but we attempt to find love in things that will kill us: pornography, promiscuous sex, and worse. We crave life-giving relationships and peace in our souls, but we settle for just about anything that provides pseudoauthenticity, pseudolife, and pseudorelationships.

Throughout my years in the counselor's chair, this destructive pattern surfaced again and again. John was married for ten years, had two kids, served in his church, and longed for greater intimacy with his wife. But he was scared—afraid to share his dreams, his hurts, his heart with the one he had committed his life to. Instead of risking vulnerability in order to have his true desires met, he instead turned to pornography and lust. Sitting in my office, he told about strippers, massage parlors, and thousands of dollars spent on Internet porn sites. And he had lost his wife and kids.

Hannah's memories of childhood sexual abuse rarely allowed her a peaceful night's sleep. Twenty-six and unmarried, she was petrified to tell her boyfriend what had happened to her. She worried that she would never be able to trust a man enough to love him. And she wondered if a man would ever truly love her. For months she had found her "peace" in anti-depressants, sleeping pills, and alcohol.

Wayne worked twelve or more hours a day, hardly ever taking a day off. He was a prominent CEO with no financial worries. When his kids grew up and left for college, his wife left him for a new life. Wayne never made it to counseling; he took his own life instead.

Wayne, Hannah, and John were locked in invisible cages that isolated them from authentic relationships. And even though they couldn't see the trap they were in, they paid the price just the same.

Here is Edward Welch's advice on identifying invisible addictions: "Look for activities or substances that entice you, leaving you wanting to come back for more, even though 'more' may not be wise, godly, or legal."[3] The things we are addicted to always leave us wanting more. Only an authentic, naked-soul encounter with another human being will leave us with the conviction that we have experienced life the way God intended.

Read and answer the following questions to differentiate between the real deal and the destructive substitute of invisible addictions.

1. As you approach the end of a stressful day, what do you find your mind looking forward to?

   a. Watching television

   b. Having a drink

   c. Getting to bed early for some extra sleep

   d. Spending time with people (family, friends)

2. When you find yourself feeling lonely and/or empty, what do you typically think of?

   a. Finding a way to have sex (or sexual release)

   b. Going to a crowded place (bar, club, gym, church)

    c. Seeking out a personal "pleasure" (anything from strenuous exercise to pornography to the use of a substance)

    d. Calling or being with someone who truly cares about you

3. When your day begins with a sense of worry and stress, how do you normally cope?

    a. I think about ways to cut people out of my schedule (by missing a family meal, a child's event, or time with a friend) so I can get more done.

    b. I experience a strange sense of energy because I know I'm good at managing tasks.

    c. I say, "Today's just like every other day."

    d. I stop to reflect and spend time with God, share my stresses with someone I'm close to, or thank God there are people who will help me through this day.

Okay, it's pretty obvious which are the life-giving options. But be honest: how many non-*d* answers describe your life?

If there is anything you regularly turn to for a sense of comfort, relief, and escape from loneliness other than God and authentic relationships with other people, then you're building walls that shut out the intimacy you crave. You must take responsibility for your life and let go of whatever addiction—pornography, lust, sex, or anything else—is substituting for authentic relationships. (I use the word *addiction* with caution, since too often we use various addictions as an excuse to avoid taking personal responsibility).

In my years as a therapist, I frequently dealt with clients who had experienced physical, sexual, and emotional abuse. Let me say as loudly as I can that the long-term effects and scars of these types of abuses are deep and heart wrenching, and it may take a very long time under good professional care to overcome the lingering consequences. You never really "get over" being the object of another person's abuse. You must understand that you were not the cause or the motivation of the abuse. Instead, you were merely the convenient target. By God's grace, you can learn to deal with the effects and reclaim your life in, for, and by God.

However, you need to avoid the other extreme: Don't use past abuse as an excuse for not taking responsibility for yourself. Don't use it as an excuse to avoid dealing with your own destructive behaviors. Both abuse and addictions can exert great power over us, but neither absolves us of personal responsibility to deal with—and to let God deal with—the hurts in our lives.

If you were abused, or if you are starting to admit that you have escapist, addictive behaviors that you need to deal with, begin your healing by finding a calm time and place to reflect. Get a journal and record your thoughts. As you spend time alone with God in His Word and in prayer, honestly ask yourself:

- What activities or things do I find myself thinking about and longing for on a frequent basis? (These could be as overt as your fear of people knowing what happened to you or the persistent wish that the abuse had never happened. Or it could be something as subtle as experiencing anxiety about talking to people, the fear of praying out loud with your mate, or rationalizing a lack of physical desire for your spouse.)

- When I am stressed and/or feeling alone, where does my mind long to be and what does my body long to do? Do I long for a drink? Do I wish I could just sit and veg out in front of the television or computer? Do I escape into sleep?

- What are my thoughts and feelings about any of these behaviors twelve hours after I indulge in them? Guilt and remorse over falling back into self-defeating behaviors? Promising myself, one more time, that I will never do it again?

- Where is God in relation to the longings of my heart? What does He want me to do differently?

As you reflect on these questions, ask God to open your eyes to the truth about yourself. And listen for His answer. Use your journal to record the insights God gives you. He wants to shatter the invisible prison that prevents you from enjoying real relationships.

GET OUT OF THE BOX

If you feel cut off from authentic relationships, you might be trapped by the prison cell sitting in the corner of your family room. They don't call television "the idiot box" for nothing. Television, more than any other influence in life, robs us of authentic relationships with others. I seriously thought about putting in several blank pages at this point and asking you to list all the ways you can think of that television robs you of authenticity. I'm fairly confident that you would have no trouble beginning such a list. However, in order to make my publisher happy, I'll go ahead and supply the background on the way television sucks the life and love out of our lives.

Unless you've been living on a desert island—one without a satellite dish—you've heard reports debating the effects of media violence on children. A position paper issued by the American Psychiatric Association states unequivocally: "The debate is over; for the last three decades, the one predominant finding in research on the mass media is that exposure to media portrayals of violence increases aggressive behavior in children."[4] And in the words of Yale psychology professor Jerome Singer: "If you came home and you found a strange man...teaching your kids to punch each other, or trying to sell them all kinds of products, you'd kick him right out of the house; but here you are, you come in and the TV is on, and you don't think twice about it."[5]

Too much television and video games, and the wrong kind of television and video games, negatively affect children. Period.

But that's the kids. We're adults, and we're mature enough to watch television in moderation and to exercise discernment in what we watch. Right? Here's the truth: While we are not as susceptible as children to media-induced tendencies toward acting out violent behavior, we do fall victim to something much more subtle. Instead of growing numb to graphic violence or human suffering, we simply become numb in general: numb to people, numb to life, numb to relationships.

Yet there is the appearance of a relationship, as seen in the viewer's eagerness to reconnect each week with the characters in his or her favorite comedy, drama, or "reality" show. Most Americans know more about the personal lives of Oprah, Jennifer Lopez, and the cast of *ER* than they do about the people who live next door or who sit beside them at church. Is that what Jesus meant by, "Love your neighbor"?

Television's portrayal of relationships is necessarily misleading. Television is a unilateral medium, whereas relationships are always bilateral. Television sets the agenda and provides all the input; the viewer has no say either in the process or the content. Television controls the script, the setting, and even dictates the emotional level of the transaction. There is no input, let alone control, from the viewer. "Wait!" you say. "I can vote with the remote." Really? How can you know and be known, how can you love and be loved, if no one is there to know you and to love you? Life and authentic relationships are never one-way. People enmeshed in the lives of television personalities fail to understand they are settling for pseudointimacy. They know all about the lives of a large number of strangers and yet become lonelier still in their real lives. There is no real relationship. It is a glass cage.

A few years back a well-known televangelist crumbled for reasons different from most. He was not found to be having a sexual affair or even embezzling money (though he enjoyed an extravagant lifestyle). Instead, his life fell apart after an investigative news team discovered that piles of letters had been thrown in the trash—checks removed, letters and prayer requests unread. And the envelopes that ministry employees determined *didn't* contain a financial contribution were tossed in the trash unopened.

Within weeks of the news report, the funds dried up. It wasn't because the evangelist was doing anything illegal. He lost the support of his followers because he was simply being inauthentic. People gave him money *because* they thought he cared and would personally pray for them. They thought this man really knew them and loved them. They were wrong. And when the truth came out, they took their money and their broken hearts elsewhere.

You might be shaking your head and thinking, "I just can't believe the gullibility of some people." You wouldn't give money to such a hypocrite, nor would you waste your time following the breathless tabloid reports on the latest on-again-off-again Hollywood romance. And you certainly don't confuse reality with the fictional lives of popular television characters. Good. But what about your viewing habits in general? Do you watch television to escape the stresses of life? Do you stretch out in the ol' Barcalounger, remote in hand, just because you need to rest and get rejuvenated for another day at work?

Author and pastor John Ortberg asks us to try to recall the last time we heard someone say, "I watched TV from the evening news to [the] late-night talk shows, and I am feeling rejuvenated, renewed, revitalized, and refreshed! What a tremendous, memorable evening that was!"[6] These words are never heard, because television provides an artificial escape, and when we return to reality, the lonely, desperate condition of our soul is just as parched as ever. Our heart yearns for authenticity, and we know that television and its surgically enhanced minions are not it.

DISCERNMENT, NOT BALANCE

You're probably wondering about my own television-viewing habits. Yes, there is a television in my home. More than one, in fact. I watch Fox News, ESPN SportsCenter with my boys (but not on school nights), local news, certain sporting events, and a few shows that my family views together if time allows. We even have family movie nights regularly. I realize that I have to monitor my "news-junkie" tendencies. I also know I'm sounding proverbially male.

The issue is not *if* we watch television (though I applaud those who choose not to), nor is the issue exclusively *what* we watch, though it's clear that we don't have carte blanche in that area. Remember Paul's standards for what we allow into our minds: "Whatever is true, whatever is noble, whatever is right, whatever is pure, whatever is lovely, whatever is admirable— if anything is excellent or praiseworthy—think about such things" (Philippians 4:8). God instructs us how to discern what we allow into our minds and how to exercise moderation in this area. But beyond *if* we watch television and *what* we watch, we need to be just as vigilant about *when* we watch.

Indulge me as I share a few facts about the average American's viewing habits:

- Seventy-five percent of Americans regularly watch television while eating dinner.
- Six million videos are rented each day, yet only three million library books are checked out daily.
- Forty-seven percent of seventh graders watch more than three hours of television daily, yet only 27 percent say they read daily for pleasure.
- Seventy-three percent of parents say they would like to limit their children's viewing. Yet, in the average American home, the set is on an average of seven hours a day.

- Fifty-four percent of four- to six-year-olds, when asked to choose between watching television and spending time with their fathers, preferred television.
- The average American child spends nine hundred hours in school each year, and fifteen hundred hours per year watching television.
- Thirty-two percent of two- to seven-year-olds have a set in their room, and two out of three kids age eight and older have one in their room.[7]

These statistics don't even address the tendency toward increased violent behavior or the studies showing the correlation between television viewing and lower reading proficiency, increased obesity, increased incidence of diabetes, and more. One of the most amazing statistics is this: "49 percent of Americans say they watch too much television."[8] Almost half of us know we're doing ourselves a disservice, yet very few of us are doing anything to change it.

Why this overindulgence in something that robs us of what we want most—soul-touching relationships with others? The answer is simple: it's much easier to turn on the tube than to share in the lives of others. In other words, it's easier to be lonely and pseudoentertained than to be loved and to love others. Watching television, even when others are in the room, can keep us in the glass cage of not being known or loved and not knowing or loving others. If the television is on, we can still be in solitary confinement.

One of the most profound things we can do for those we love is simply push the Off button. Ever since our first child was born fourteen years ago, my wife and I have made a simple commitment and enforced a simple rule. The commitment is that we will make eating dinner together as a family a priority, and the rule is that the television will *not* be on while we eat. Instead, we either play "High/Low" (where each person shares the "high" event of the day and the "low" event of the day), or we have a "question of the day." Sometimes we just talk about whatever is on everyone's mind. Those are cherished times in our family.

These things don't take place without planning and effort. My kids are involved in all the activities of normal kids. So at times, it means not having dinner until 7:00 p.m. when everyone gets home. There may be some inconvenience in meal preparation and kid shuffling, but the higher priority is to be *together in an authentic way.* To make authentic relationships happen, you first have to be together. And second, you have to push the Off button on the remote.

We need to disconnect from the television. Then we need to engage one another in conversation or play a board game, go for a walk, play tennis, or engage in some other activity that will help draw people out. We need to live with new, life-giving priorities.

"I Don't Do TV; I IM"

I would be remiss if I didn't address the video monitor of choice among teenagers: the computer screen. According to the Pew Internet and American Life Project, 74 percent of teenagers in the United States aged twelve to seventeen use the Internet. Of those seventeen million youth, 74 percent use instant messaging (IM), compared to only 44 percent of adults who use the Internet. Nearly seven in ten Internet-using teenagers use IM at least several times a week.[9]

Just as I didn't propose that we hold a "television burning" in the church parking lot, neither do I advise abolishing the Internet or even IM-ing. There are many good things about both. I do, however, have a grave warning: Sending an instant message—or even an e-mail—is not the same as authentic communication. It's one dimensional; people are not.

It is also incredibly easy to be cruel. It is common for people using IM to send snide, hurtful, and vindictive messages. Sender A says something malicious to Sender B about Sender C, knowing that Sender C and a dozen other folks are reading it online. As a counselor and as a parent I have heard examples of dozens of teens saying stuff online that they would never have the courage (or the cruelty) to say to someone in person.

IM-ing can be cool. Text messaging can be fun. But believing it is authentic communication is wrong. Thinking it is always harmless is wrong as well. The thirst of loneliness will never be quenched in the single-dimension world of the Internet.

COMMUNICATION, THEN COMMUNION

The great preacher Dr. Haddon Robinson used to say that one of the most important questions we must answer, when it comes to our prayer life, is simply, why pray? Part of his answer was that we pray so there can be two-way communication with God. "Without communication," he explained, "there can be no communion; and without communion, there can be no relationship."[10] As C. S. Lewis is quoted as saying: "I do not pray because it changes God; I pray because it changes me."[11] We pray to communicate; we pray to know and to be known.

Author and philosophy professor Dallas Willard echoes this theme: "When communication between two people rises to the level of communion, there is distinctness but also a profound sharing of the thoughts, feelings, and objectives that make up our lives. Each recognizes the thought or feeling as his or hers, while knowing with joy that the other is feeling or thinking in the same way."[12]

Our soul does not long only for communication, although there is great value in the exchange of information. We yearn for more. We seek true communion—with God and with others. Sadly, however, we think we'll find the deep connection of communion in a variety of dead-end behaviors. There is no real communion in pornography or casual sex. There is no real communion in watching television or surfing the Internet or exchanging instant messages.

Communion requires authentic, two-way, face-to-face encounters. In spite of the risk, what we truly long for is someone to see our naked soul— not for their entertainment but so we can experience God's amazing, everyday solution to loneliness. We want to find a way to take the risk of emotional and spiritual nakedness so we can be known and loved by others.

Without communication, there is no communion.

Without communion, there is no relationship.

Without relationships, there is no love.

And without love, we have nothing to look forward to but more loneliness.

Reflection

The Big Idea

God designed each of us for authentic relationships with other people. Relationships require communion, and communion requires communication. Yet far too often we settle for artificial communication, communion, and relationships because we have immersed ourselves in a variety of mind-numbing behaviors, including staring at our "entertainment center" and having sex for the sake of pleasure. God calls us to love full-dimensionally, which demands that we make the time to sit and talk, face to face, without interruption.

Key Verse

"Finally, brethren, whatever is true, whatever is honorable, whatever is right, whatever is pure, whatever is lovely, whatever is of good repute, if there is any excellence and if anything worthy of praise, dwell on these things." (Philippians 4:8, NASB)

Answering Questions

- Are you involved in the escapist activities of too much television watching or casual sex (or sex aimed at personal pleasure rather than oneness with your spouse)? If so, what is your invisible prison? Do the hard work of writing down the answer.
- Are you ready to break out of the cage, to free yourself from the negative effects and find true relationships? If so, what are you willing to change and when? If not, why not?
- Are you ready to experience the love that can never come through television or casual sex? Great. That's what God wants for you. Write out your plan for the changes you are going to make, and share your plan with a close friend.

Prayer

Loving Lord, it is so easy to turn to things—rather than turn to You—in my attempts to find peace and connection. And yet, in reality, "things" serve only to numb my pain, providing temporary escape and driving me further from You. God, by Your grace and love, help me turn always to You. Bring into my life the people with whom I can have true communion. Help me to take the risk *now* to truly love and listen to the people You have put in my life. Lord God, help me to love others in naked-soul relationships. Amen.

Eight

Selfishness, Security, and Stagnation

The Life That Guarantees Your Loneliness

> Only two things are infinite, the universe and human stupidity;
> and I'm not sure about the former.
>
> —ALBERT EINSTEIN

I n the fall of 2003 actor Arnold Schwarzenegger was made governor of California in a recall election. President George W. Bush appeared with the governor-elect a few weeks later and commented on similarities between the two men. "We both married well," the president said. "Some accuse us both of not being able to speak the language. We both have big biceps. Well, two out of three isn't bad."[1]

Good speech writing. Healthy self-deprecation. And I know exactly what the president was talking about. Like these two men, I married well. In fact, not only did I marry well, I married *way* over my head.

It's healthy for us to remind ourselves of the blessing that we have in our spouses and our closest friends, since our natural tendency is to focus on ourselves and minimize the importance of other people in our lives. In other words, we're selfish.

As a marriage counselor, a theologian, and a bumbling husband, I can assure you that the greatest problem in marriage is *not* disagreements about money, differences in a couple's sex drive, the stress of careers, or issues related to raising kids. Those are just the most frequent things couples fight about. The greatest problem in marriage is that we get ticked off and start fights because we don't get what we want when we want it. Our problem is that we're selfish.

The first sin in the Garden of Eden teaches us as much about pride and selfishness as it does about disobeying God. Adam and Eve didn't like being told what they could and could not do. They didn't like Someone else limiting their options. They were adults, after all. They could manage just fine on their own. In their pride they chose to disobey, and their egoistic desires led them away from God. As James wrote:

> When tempted, no one should say, "God is tempting me." For
> God cannot be tempted by evil, nor does he tempt anyone; but
> each one is tempted when, by his own evil desire, he is dragged
> away and enticed. Then, after desire has conceived, it gives
> birth to sin; and sin, when it is full-grown, gives birth to death.
> (James 1:13–15)

In the garden, humans were selfish. In James's day two thousand years ago, humans were selfish. It's the same today. If we were looking for the basic reasons why we don't experience life-changing relationships that overcome our loneliness, we would find selfishness, security, and stagnation at the top of the list.

THREE STUPID CHOICES

Humans are so shortsighted that they often invest great energy in doing the very things that guarantee failure. I know I've starred in that movie more than once. When it comes to the pain of being alone, we regularly make three choices that prolong our loneliness and prevent us from really knowing others and being known by others.

The Blindness of Selfishness

Most of us are blind to our selfishness, at least most of the time, because it comes so naturally to us. We are inherently selfish (anyone who has children knows whose needs an infant cares about), so our natural tendency is to be more concerned about ourselves and less concerned about the needs and desires of others. Sorry, I don't buy the *tabla rasa* or "blank slate" theory. We are born selfish. The traits of a maturing individual include the ability to sincerely care about the needs of another person, and not just what the other person can do for us. But our natural bent wars against authentic relationships, since such relationships require us to consciously sacrifice our selfishness for the well-being of others.

The Lure of Security

The absence of authentic relationships creates loneliness, but we fail to see authentic relationships as the *solution* to our loneliness. We feel more secure pursuing artificial substitutes. Many of us choose safety over risk, so we refuse to leave the security of the known to venture into the unknown territory of reaching out to others. The irony of clinging to our own security is that it keeps us insecure and alone.

The Deadening Choice of Stagnation

When a person becomes stagnant, he simply decides to quit growing spiritually, emotionally, and relationally. Often the person doesn't realize he has made that choice. The English word *stagnant* comes from the Latin word *stagnum,* meaning "swamp." When water becomes trapped, without an inlet to receive fresh water, it becomes stagnant, meaning that it is "dead water," lacking in vitality and healthy life. It even begins to stink. When a person fails to grow, he fails to reach out to others, and his life loses vitality and health. The result is loneliness. And loneliness stinks.

THE RICH YOUNG POSTER CHILD

Jesus offered hard advice to a man who took comfort in having a lot of stuff. Jesus's advice, simply put, was, "If you wish to be complete, go and sell your possessions and give to the poor, and you will have treasure in heaven; and come, follow Me" (Matthew 19:21, NASB). This wasn't what the man wanted to hear. The Bible records that the young man "went away grieving; for he was one who owned much property" (19:22, NASB).

The nameless man, who has come to be known simply as the rich young ruler, serves as a consummate example of a life of selfishness, security, and stagnation. The whole story reads:

> A certain ruler asked him, "Good teacher, what must I do to
> inherit eternal life?"
>
> "Why do you call me good?" Jesus answered. "No one is
> good—except God alone. You know the commandments: 'Do

not commit adultery, do not murder, do not steal, do not give false testimony, honor your father and mother.'"

"All these I have kept since I was a boy," he said.

When Jesus heard this, he said to him, "You still lack one thing. Sell everything you have and give to the poor, and you will have treasure in heaven. Then come, follow me."

When he heard this, he became very sad, because he was a man of great wealth. Jesus looked at him and said, "How hard it is for the rich to enter the kingdom of God! Indeed, it is easier for a camel to go through the eye of a needle than for a rich man to enter the kingdom of God."

Those who heard this asked, "Who then can be saved?"

Jesus replied, "What is impossible with men is possible with God." (Luke 18:18–27)

Like Adam and Eve, this young man had the remarkable opportunity to ask God a question face to face. He heard God tell him the difference between right and wrong and the way he should live. And like Adam and Eve, this self-absorbed man chose to go his own way. He cared more about himself than he did about authentically loving God and others. Even his claim that he had kept all of God's commandments since he "was a boy" is more about himself than God. He obeyed just so he could look good and say that he obeyed. He was, like you and me, selfish. And he relied on himself for a sense of security.

Need proof? Notice that he balked when it came to shifting his focus from himself to others. He was more concerned about himself and, specifically, his own security. His being a rich dude and a ruler gave him security in life. To go, sell, give, and follow—as Jesus commanded—would have forced him to shift his focus away from himself. He was good at trusting himself to follow the commandments, at least in the way they were defined prior to Christ's teachings. But he wasn't good at trusting God. Instead, he derived his security from his station in life. What would people think of him if he were no longer rich?

And what about the stagnant part? Even as this man approached the "good teacher" with a question, it's clear that he was not ready to grow. Every parent has had the experience of a child asking a question, knowing already the answer the child wants to hear. But when the parent says, "Yes, you must eat all your brussels sprouts" and "No, you absolutely cannot climb up on the roof and jump into the wading pool like Jimmy McDermott did" (they usually don't ask questions like the last one until *after* the fact), the child often becomes "very sad" (Luke 18:23). It's part of the immaturity of being a kid. But as adults, getting answers we don't like to hear—especially when those answers are the truth coming from God—also causes us to become sad. We're just not ready to grow up. We prefer to stay where we are and grow more stagnant.

Jesus said, "No one who puts his hand to the plow and looks back is fit for service in the kingdom of God" (Luke 9:62). John wrote, "If anyone has material possessions and sees his brother in need but has no pity on him, how can the love of God be in him?" (1 John 3:17). And God said: "You shall not make for yourself an idol in the form of anything in heaven above or on the earth beneath or in the waters below. You shall not bow down to them or worship them; for I, the LORD your God, am a jealous God, punishing the children for the sin of the fathers to the third and fourth generation of those who hate me, but showing love to a thousand generations of those who love me and keep my commandments" (Exodus 20:4–6).

Keeping all of God's commandments includes loving God. Loving God involves doing what God says. Doing what God says involves authentically loving the people God brings across our paths. Loving people authentically means dealing with our selfishness, our misguided understanding of security, and our stagnation.

SLAYING THE SELFISH DRAGON

As I was driving into Washington DC a few years ago, I saw what has become one of my favorite road signs. It read: Road Construction Ahead: Prepare to Be Aggravated. I like it for its humor, its honesty, and for its role in fulfilling the Boy Scout motto: Be Prepared. Knowing that aggravation is coming enables us to deal with the frustrations in a healthier way. And in case you don't know, it is coming.

When the alarm goes off in the morning, and we drag our weary bodies out of bed, it would be great if there were two road signs replete with flashing lights to prepare us for the day. The first would read: Life Ahead: Remember, God Loves You and Has a Purpose for You Today. The second sign would read: People Ahead: Prepare to Be Aggravated.

We don't like it when people interrupt the smooth operation of our lives. It's really aggravating. But why? Because we're selfish. Our self-centeredness doesn't cause frustrating things to happen, but it does produce the artery-tightening, fist-clinching, vein-popping reaction in our bodies. We believe deep in our being that frustrating things should happen to other people, but not to *us*.

When it's stated that way, it's easy to see the flaw in the logic. But just because it's an erroneous belief doesn't reduce its effect on our lives. Rational emotive therapy is a psychological school of thought that underscores the crucial role played by our beliefs. What we believe about a circumstance determines how we will react to it. Many believe that when an event or precipitating action (A=action) happens, they in turn respond (C=emotional consequence) directly to that event. The reaction can be happiness or anger or indifference. But no matter what the reaction is, they believe it's caused by the event.

They are wrong. In truth, what causes the response is not the event itself, but rather what we believe (B=believe) about the event. The intensity of our response is directly proportional to what we believe about the precipitating action.

Picture yourself driving down a road at the posted speed limit of forty-five miles per hour when a car pulls in front of you while exiting a fast-food restaurant parking lot. You are forced to hit your brakes to avoid running up the backside of the guy's SUV. How do you react? Do you scream, honk, gesture? Do you laugh about it, pray about it, or speed up so you can pass him and give him a wilting glare? Do you stop to consider that the guy might be having a really bad day? Do you take the incident in stride, concluding that if his reckless driving doesn't kill him, eating that junk food will?

Seriously, what is your response? And what caused your response?

Most people in this situation would feel angry, and they would blame their anger on the other driver. "I'm mad because that self-centered idiot pulled out in front of me!" But that's not completely true. What caused your reaction, and mine, is what we believe about people who have the gall to pull out in front of us.

Do we believe that having to hit our brakes to avoid a collision is simply part of the driving experience? If so, when it happens, we just slow down because it's part of safe driving. There is no anger attached to it.

Or do your reactions instead show that you believe you should never have to alter your course or slow your progress while driving due to the actions of other motorists? If you hold this view, then your reaction will involve angry words, a honking horn, and the self-assessed "appropriate" glare and hand gestures. Judging by the volatility of some drivers, they must believe that the other driver waited all day at the drive-through exit until *they* came along so he could victimize *them and only them.*

And it's not just that we get aggravated in traffic. Am I justified in yelling at the clerk who messed up *my* order, the co-worker who was late and made *me* rush to meet a deadline, or the waiter who served the people at the next table but was slow in bringing *my* food? Do I understand that the rest of humanity is not here for my convenience?

All right, let's talk about aggravation. This is the second time I've written this chapter. I had it finished when I decided to swap out the batteries in my laptop. Even though I saved the document before switching batteries, when I booted back up, I couldn't find the file. Auto-recovery didn't help. Auto-save was useless. Why was this happening to *me?* Well, in this case it's because God has a great sense of humor and had to remind me in the midst of my ranting that computer demons apply to *me,* too; life's inconveniences happen to me. These things apply to you, too. Are we appropriately prepared for them?

We need to get over ourselves. God did not say, "Go and yell at all those who make your life miserable." He said for us to go out there and "carry each other's burdens, and in this way you will fulfill the law of Christ" (Galatians 6:2). If I don't let God deal with my egocentric approach to life, I will never love and be loved or know and be known. And the only world I will care about will be the one that I like to think revolves around me, and that is a very lonely place.

A man once stood before a crowd and said, "Look, Lord! Here and now I give half of my possessions to the poor, and if I have cheated anybody out of anything, I will pay back four times the amount." Jesus said to this guy, "Today salvation has come to this house, because this man, too, is a son of Abraham. For the Son of Man came to seek and to save what was lost" (Luke 19:8–10). Zacchaeus finally realized that his own concerns and his financial security were not paramount. Instead, he came to believe that God had prior claim on his life. Over lunch with the Son of God, his life was completely changed.

And notice the outcome. He didn't say, "Look, Lord, I'm going to go to church more, pray more, be a better person." There is nothing wrong with any of those things, but Zacchaeus's first reaction was not to do things that would make him look more "righteous." Instead, his first desire was to obey God by correcting the injustices he had committed against others. He wanted to take care of others, not himself. He gave up his wealth and paid back those he had cheated.

When God invades our life, one of the first things He deals with is our selfishness. And there is a reason for that: we can't love others and truly change the world until we let the green dragon of "me first, me most" come face to face with God—and be destroyed. We must begin to die to ourselves.

Did Zacchaeus ever have another selfish thought or do another selfish thing in the days and years following? Absolutely. But unlike the rich young ruler, Zacchaeus was willing to go God's way. He gave up the earthly things he relied on, and he started loving others as Christ loves us. Our worldview must begin with a clear view of God and His rule over us.

TRADING OUR FALSE SECURITY

A widely told story about an unemployed acrobat helps us understand some of the ways we rely on false security. It seems a down-on-his-luck acrobat was desperate for work, so he scanned the want ads. There were few openings for acrobats, but one prospect caught his eye: "Man with Acrobatic Skills Needed at Zoo."

He rushed to interview for the job. As he spoke with the manager, he found that instead of performing as an acrobat, they wanted him to wear a gorilla suit and pretend to be a gorilla by leaping and climbing and swinging around the gorilla pen. The zoo's gorilla had died, and they couldn't afford a new one. The acrobat wasn't thrilled with the arrangement but felt he had no choice. "One more thing," the manager told him. "You must always remain in character and don't let any of the patrons know what you really are."

It didn't take long before the acrobat was playing the part perfectly, keeping the crowds entertained. But one day he tired of the routine, and as he swung from one branch to the next, not giving it his full attention, he missed a limb and sailed over the wall, landing in the lions' compound.

Fearing for his life, the acrobat began to scream, "Help! Help me! I'm going to be eaten." In response to the screams, the lion leaned over and whispered to the frightened man, "If you don't shut up, we're both going to lose our jobs."

Too many of us waste our lives pretending to be somebody we're not. We believe that if we are truly known, we will be rejected and found unlovable. We hide who we really are, thinking it will bring us security. And we are as lonely as ever.

Ananias and his wife, Sapphira, were selfish but didn't want to look that way, so they conspired to hide the truth from God and Peter. It cost them their lives (Acts 5). Adam and Eve were ashamed of their sin and nakedness and hid from God. Jesus made it clear that we are the light of the world and that we should never hide our light. But we do.

God said,

> Am I only a God nearby…
>   and not a God far away?
> Can anyone hide in secret places
>   so that I cannot see him?…
> Do not I fill heaven and earth? (Jeremiah 23:23–24)

Trying to hide from God is never a good strategy. Neither is hiding from other people. Adam and Eve tried it; we've all tried it. Certainly there are people who would exploit or humiliate us if they knew our secrets and hidden struggles. We must be wise in how we share deep personal secrets and with whom. But we must also be bold and willing to share who we really are and receive comfort from those who struggle as we do. We need to be reminded of this truth: "No test or temptation that comes your way is beyond the course of what others have had to face. All you need to remember is that God will never let you down; he'll never let you be pushed past your limit; he'll always be there to help you come through it" (1 Corinthians 10:13, MSG). There is only one way we can experience the power of that verse, and that is in being real with others.

We need to experience the healing that is promised in James's words: "Make this your common practice: Confess your sins to each other and pray for each other so that you can live together whole and healed. The prayer of a person living right with God is something powerful to be reckoned with" (James 5:16, MSG). We find the healing power of that verse by becoming authentic with people.

Security is never found in trying to keep our true selves hidden from God or others. Real security is not found in our jobs, our bank accounts, our abilities, or our looks. Jesus said, "There is nothing concealed that will not be disclosed, or hidden that will not be made known" (Luke 12:2). He criticized the Pharisees for justifying themselves in the eyes of other people—pretending on the outside to be someone they weren't on the inside. He reminded them that "God knows your hearts" (Luke 16:15). Security is not found in a facade or in this world.

Real security comes from knowing and trusting God. We'll all land in the lions' den one day, disguised as something we're not, and, truth is, we'll be surrounded by other fakes too, fearing for our lives. We must know that God is the only One who can pull us out to a place of safety and security.

REFUSING TO SUBMIT TO STAGNATION

You can give my wonderful mother a stick, a little dirt, and a plastic container, and she can turn it into one of the most beautiful African violets you've ever seen. That's a talent I didn't inherit, and neither did my wife. Still, I'm the designated caretaker of the few pitiable plants we keep around our house. There's not much I know about it except for this (and you can take this to the bank): to survive and grow, a plant must have water and light. It's not quantum physics; it is just life for a plant.

We know that our bodies will die without food, water, air, and sleep. But we forget that our souls also need certain things for survival. The death of a soul is harder to see. But it begins with stagnation, when no real love is flowing in or out.

It seems Christians have the unique ability to go to church, go to Bible studies, hang around with other believers, and still never change. We can say our prayers and make resolutions every New Year's Eve and Ash Wednesday and yet somehow emerge on the other side unscathed by anything good or bad. If we don't let real words from God and real relationships with others flow into our hearts and souls, then our hearts and souls will become stale. They will stagnate.

Over the last twelve years I've had a front-row seat to observe what I'll call "the stagnation of Harry." I've changed enough of the story to assure his privacy, but Harry is a real person. I've never professionally counseled Harry or his family. I never played the role of their pastor (they went to a different church). I tried on numerous occasions to be his friend, but there was never an open door.

By all outward appearances, Harry and his wife were happy and successful. In the early years they were at church fairly frequently, volunteered occasionally at church events, and were open to discussing spiritual things. They spoke of wanting to have children, serving in the church, and building their futures together.

Then life showed up. Kids came with all the demands, distractions, and confusion that kids bring. Then in-law problems invaded. With his career on the fast track, Harry was named the youngest-ever CEO of a growing company. But then work problems invaded his life. Lawsuits were filed, and Harry had to fight to clear his name. And on it goes.

During these years Harry's involvement in church as well as his willingness to seek counsel from others dwindled to zero. His wife and children tried to come to services, but he worked. People tried to care, and he hid.

It would be impossible to map all the pain, problems, money grabs, fights, and affairs in Harry's marriage and family life. His marriage eventually ended in divorce. From the outside, you might be tempted to conclude that the deck was stacked against him. He had so much to deal with, he just got buried by the circumstances. But if you knew Harry and bothered to look into his heart, you'd see a different story. With each stressful event of life, Harry pulled more and more inside himself. He shut out everyone from his parents to his children to his wife to his friends to his church. He quit growing. Oh, he might have grown in his knowledge of operating a business, but his soul, his ability to relate to those who cared about him, shriveled up. He made every decision with the subconscious intent of trying to protect himself from hurt. Every attempt by other people to reach out to him was met with a polite smile—and a wall.

Stagnant souls do not let people in, and they don't come clean before God. Those with stagnant hearts don't realize that in pushing people away, they are sealing themselves off from the lifeline that God sends them. God and the people who care about us are the only remedies to a stagnant soul.

DON'T BE STUPID

We all make mistakes, we all goof up, and we all fall short of the glory of God. We make stupid decisions that end up hurting ourselves and others. And one of the saddest choices is when people are given the insight and ability to do something that will vastly improve their life—that will bring an end to loneliness—and they still choose *not* to do it.

When I was a therapist, I'd often give a couple or an individual an assignment that I *knew* would put the person or the marriage on the road to recovery, yet they would fail to do it. Then they'd get upset that things were not getting better. This must be how medical doctors feel when they advise a patient to change his diet and to get more exercise, and he chooses a heart attack over a change of lifestyle.

When we are given wisdom based on God's truth and proven fact, and we still choose to ignore it, that's just stupid. It's what Adam and Eve did. It's what you and I have done from time to time.

So let's wise up. Our souls cry out to know and be known, to love and be loved. Our heart yearns to live a life that matters to God and to others. We long to have an impact on the world. The time is right to lay hold of those dreams.

It begins with tearing down the walls we've built around our hearts. It involves slowing down, being silent before God, praying, reflecting on God's Word. It requires that we become more concerned about others than we are about ourselves. It demands that we take big risks, leaving the false security of self-protection so we can entrust ourselves to God's protection as we engage in authentic relationships with other people.

The Bible says, "We want to live well, but our foremost efforts should be to help *others* live well" (1 Corinthians 10:24, MSG). The Bible says, "Don't be obsessed with getting your own advantage. Forget yourselves long enough to lend a helping hand" (Philippians 2:4, MSG).

Jesus said, "If your first concern is to look after yourself, you'll never find yourself. But if you forget about yourself and look to me, you'll find both yourself and me" (Matthew 10:39, MSG). He also said, "Self-help is no help at all. Self-sacrifice is the way, *my* way, to finding yourself, your true self" (Luke 9:24, MSG).

To refuse to listen to the Lord of life about how we should live is, well, stupid.

And it's not just stupid. It's a guarantee of loneliness.

Let's let go of loneliness and grab on to real life.

Reflection

The Big Idea

We all struggle with being selfish, with wanting our lives to be safe and secure, and with getting into hectic ruts that ultimately cause us to stagnate. To live truly authentic lives, God calls us to slay all three of these dragons. We are to minister to the needs of others. We are to get our need for security filled in God and God alone. And we all need to keep the stream of living water from God flowing into our life so that we grow more and more into His likeness.

Key Verse

"When Jesus heard this, he said to him, 'You still lack one thing. Sell everything you have and give to the poor, and you will have treasure in heaven. Then come, follow me.'" (Luke 18:22)

Answering Questions

- After considering the issues of selfishness, security, and stagnation in your life, what do you find? Write down thoughts about areas in your life that you believe God is calling you to work on.

- Are you willing to take the risk of coming out of hiding so you can find true security by trusting God, and God alone? Prayerfully tell God how you are going to do that. Ask for His help. Write down your plan and commit it to Him.

- Are you ready to take the risk of looking past your own needs and reaching out to other people? Are you ready to live God's way? What's preventing you? Will you react like the rich young ruler, or will you follow Jesus in looking out for the welfare of others and not just your own welfare?

Prayer

Loving Lord, since the Garden of Eden, Your children have struggled with being selfish, with looking to ourselves and our "protective walls" for security, and with worrying about our own little worlds more than trusting You. Help me to break free from these vain toils. Give me the faith to trust Your Word and then to live a life of significance that focuses on loving and serving You and loving and serving others. Bless my life, Lord, so I can be a blessing to others. Amen.

Nine

Getting Real with God

What It Means to Follow God in Authentic Relationship

In accepting what God wills for us

do we find our peace.

—Dante Alighieri

A s I sit down to finish writing this chapter, I'm having difficulty focusing. It's the Lenten season, and earlier today my wife and I went to see the movie *The Passion of the Christ.* I am haunted by images.

It's not just the extent of the torture that Jesus endured. I've studied the details of first-century scourgings and crucifixions, so I was prepared for the film's portrayal of these barbaric acts. Still, seeing it in such detail on the big screen moved me to tears and made me feel I was present to witness the greatest display of grace there has ever been.

However, what haunts me is not so much the heartrending depiction of the mock trial and the prolonged suffering of Jesus. The thing that is lodged in my heart and that I can't get out of my mind is the unadulterated authenticity of the incarnate Son of God. The physical suffering He endured was not minimized in the slightest degree. His fear was authentic. His questions to His Father were authentic. His pain was authentic. His love for us and His obedience to God were authentic.

His relationship with God was authentic.

The Authentic Prayer

Prayer is a gift to us, because God graciously invites us to regularly, authentically pour out our hearts to Him. We are completely free to make known our needs, our desires, our hopes, our sins, and our dependence on Him. Prayer is communion with the One who loves us most.

In a chapel address at Denver Seminary years ago, Dr. Haddon Robinson compared prayer in the life of Jesus to that of most of us. In our lives, prayer is often used as preparation for the battle—no matter what the battles in our life may be. For Jesus, prayer was the battle itself. Haddon stated that, for Jesus, prayer was like studying for exams, and ministry was walking across the stage for the diploma. Prayer to our Lord was like training for a marathon; ministry was walking onto the podium to receive the gold medal.

Dr. Robinson surmises that if you had seen Christ in the Garden of Gethsemane, you would have thought, "If He is agonizing like this now, when He is simply in prayer by Himself, what's He going to be like when the real test comes in Jerusalem? What will happen to Him when He faces the questions of Pilate and Herod? What will He do when confronted with death?" You might have even wondered why He couldn't be more like His sleeping friends, who did not, at first, seem as worried as He was. But wait. When the test actually came, when He stood before the crowd who cried out, "Crucify Him!" it was Jesus who went to the cross in victory, and it was His sleeping friends who fell away and ran away.

As the Gethsemane scene ends in *The Passion of the Christ*, and Jesus arises from His agonizing prayer, His face is no longer in pain but rather shows an aura of triumphant victory. I thought of Dr. Robinson's message; the battle was over.

Graduation day.

BEING REAL IN PRAYER

When you come before the God of the universe in prayer, what is your attitude and mind-set? I must admit that there are far too many times when my prayers are anything but authentic. I'm way too casual about the shape of my soul. I'm in a hurry to get on to more "important" things. And I'm often asking God to save me from situations that I created myself.

If I am to be real in this hurting world—real with other people—I must first get real before my Creator. If I think I can bare my soul to others while hiding the condition of my soul from God, I am deceived. Step one in being real is to be real before God's throne.

Much too often, I believe, we falsely pass off the events and circumstances of our lives as "God's will." It's a way of blaming God for certain circumstances so we won't have to accept responsibility for our own failures. When we wrongly point the finger at God, we are inauthentic before the One who is anything but.

Too many people walk away from their marriages because they are bored or "just not happy." They cut and run before their "last chance at a fulfilling life is gone forever." Scared to be real with God about their sins and weaknesses, they instead attribute their broken commitments to God's will. "God wants me to be happy, and I can't be happy in my current marriage." I honestly can't count how many times I've heard this line from dear, hurting, confused, and wrong people.

But it doesn't end with blaming God for broken relationships. I've heard others attribute all sorts of negative life circumstances to God's sovereign will. A pastor friend recently told me about having to let a staff member go because he wasn't doing his job. Instead of getting angry or demanding that he be given another chance, the fired employee simply said, "Well, it must be God's will." My friend had desired a more authentic response.

People blame God for everything from getting fired to "having" to accept a new job that requires a family move. Everything from not having any close friends to moving in with a girlfriend or boyfriend. Everything from mishandled finances to an extramarital affair to a serious illness to having to endure a miserable, boring, lonely life.

Take your pick, we're quick to blame God. But are these *really* God's will?

Chalking up life's reversals to the will of the Almighty is a cop-out. Blaming God for *our* failures makes us puppets, and there is no relational authenticity in a puppet. God wants us to engage Him in the give-and-take of a real relationship. Getting angry about adverse circumstances is real. Demanding answers or seeking an explanation is real. Looking inside ourselves to try to identify attitudes or behaviors that contribute to life's setbacks is real. Accepting responsibility is real. Obedience to God is real. Seeking to follow God faithfully is real. None of this is easy, but all of it is real.

God understands that, and He doesn't leave us on our own. He gives us what we need to pull it off. Still, we unnecessarily complicate our lives and invite pain when we could easily avoid it by living in obedience to God's requirements. For example, if we accept the Bible as God's Word, then there is no gray area when it comes to sexual purity. Paul made it clear: "But among you there must not be even a hint of sexual immorality, or of any kind of impurity, or of greed, because these are improper for God's holy people" (Ephesians 5:3).

We don't need to engage in a debate over what qualifies or does not qualify as sexual immorality. We're to keep our distance from even a hint of impurity. And in obeying this teaching, we are also protecting ourselves from the pain of being violated, being used, and being betrayed by others who are seeking their own sexual gratification. And that doesn't even touch on the physical and emotional benefits of sexual purity.

Yes, life is hard. Yes, we need help. So how can we be real before God when it comes to the struggles that threaten to bury us?

BACK TO THE GARDEN

Jesus didn't attempt to hide how He felt. "'*Abba,* Father,' he said, 'everything is possible for you. Take this cup from me'" (Mark 14:36). In calling God both *Abba* and *Father,* Jesus used the Aramaic and the Greek forms of the word. He was expressing a submissive spirit as the Son and also the endearing, loving, pleading cry of a desperate child wanting His Dad to help Him. It is the cry I have heard hundreds of times as my children have screamed for me in every situation from broken bones to bloody knees to fear of falling to fear of anything else. They scream "Daddy!" because they know *and* believe that Daddy can and will help them.

Jesus knew that His Daddy could save Him. When Jesus was more frightened than He had ever been, He turned to His Daddy. I must imagine that God's first desire was to reach down and pick up His Son and comfort Him. Jesus had taught about the natural inclination of fathers to care for their children: "Which of you, if his son asks for bread, will give him a stone? Or if he asks for a fish, will give him a snake?" (Matthew 7:9–10).

Just a few days ago there was a nonstop ringing of our doorbell. I went to the door expecting to find one of the neighbor children or one of my own kids being goofy and too lazy to go around to the open garage door.

159

What I found was my eleven-year-old, Caleb, sprawled on the porch where he had managed to drag his bruised and bleeding body after crashing on his skateboard. It took only a nanosecond to go from a "who's goofing around with the doorbell" attitude to the "I'm a dad, and my son needs me" posture. When his eyes pleaded for help, I couldn't imagine refusing to do everything I could to help him.

Jesus knew that His Father could help Him. God could spare Him this ordeal. Yet Jesus said, "Not what I will, but what you will" (Mark 14:36). We have no record of what God said in response. We have no idea what God was feeling at that moment. But if there was ever a time that the heart of God was breaking, this was it. If there was ever a moment when a war was raging in heaven over issues of love, obedience, and a desire to do something other than what the ultimate love of the Father demanded, it was *this* moment.

What we do know is that Jesus walked back to his sleeping friends and said, "Are you still sleeping and resting? Enough! The hour has come. Look, the Son of Man is betrayed into the hands of sinners" (Mark 14:41). We know He lived authentically. We know He prayed authentically. And we know He finished His life authentically by obediently going to the cross.

And we know that Jesus laid out the requirements for us to live authentically: "If anyone would come after me, he must deny himself and take up his cross daily and follow me" (Luke 9:23).

AUTHENTIC OBEDIENCE

Stan has been my longtime friend and mentor. During my early days of faith in Christ, I remember Stan telling stories of when he was reading the Old Testament for the first time. He would read descriptions of war such as this:

So Joshua subdued the whole region, including the hill country,
the Negev, the western foothills and the mountain slopes,
together with all their kings. He left no survivors. He totally
destroyed all who breathed, just as the LORD, the God of Israel,
had commanded. (Joshua 10:40)

Stan would get so angry that he'd throw his Bible across the room and
scream, "How could You, a God of love, do something like that? How
could You just order that all of those people be destroyed?"

How do you reconcile a loving God with such a command? Do you
simply cruise past it, thinking, *That was another time, and God must have
had His reasons that we just can't understand?* Or do you, out of love for
humankind, question God and share your hurts and confusion and even
your anger? Are you able to be real before God?

Stan was not (and is not to this day) scared to ask God the hard questions, nor is he afraid to bring his true emotions before the throne of the
Creator. I must also say that Stan is one of the most "take up your cross and
follow me" men that I know, constantly going to talk with people about
what it means to love Jesus. To be authentic before God is to be authentic
in *every* area of life. It is to live out the first and greatest commandment, to
"Love the Lord your God with all your heart and with all your soul and
with all your mind and with all your strength" (Mark 12:30). Loving God
involves our thoughts, our feelings, our actions, and our soul's deepest
yearnings. Jesus didn't say we could pick just one; it's a package deal.

WE'RE NOT GOD

Steven Curtis Chapman has a gift for putting into song the thoughts and
feelings that so many of us struggle with. Writing in response to the tragic,

soul-wrenching death of a friend's child, attempting to find both answers and comfort, Chapman simply and profoundly sings, "God is God, and I am not."[1]

It's one of the lessons that Job learned.

> Then the LORD answered Job out of the storm. He said:
>
> "Who is this that darkens my counsel
>   with words without knowledge?
> Brace yourself like a man;
>   I will question you,
>   and you shall answer me.
>
> "Where were you when I laid the earth's foundation?
>   Tell me, if you understand.
> Who marked off its dimensions? Surely you know!
>   Who stretched a measuring line across it?
> On what were its footings set,
>   or who laid its cornerstone—
> while the morning stars sang together
>   and all the angels shouted for joy?" (Job 38:1–7)

Sometimes people believe that the adage "be a man" or "act like a man" is nothing more than a sexist, anti-emotion reprimand to someone who is not behaving in a tough, "manly" manner. Maybe. But I find it interesting that God uses it here. Job is told by God to brace himself "like a man," to get ready for something really hard. Get ready, Job, to answer for all your words, for all your attempts to explain God's actions. You'd better be prepared and be strong because you, Job, are about to be questioned by God Himself.

If you're unfamiliar with the story, Job was a servant of God and a very wealthy man. At the request of Satan himself, God allowed (He did not directly cause) Job to go through numerous painful trials that included loss of family, loss of wealth, and loss of health. It is instructive that in God's discussion with Job, He did not explain *why* all this was happening. Instead, through His questions, God demonstrated that since a human can never fully comprehend the origin and establishment of God's natural laws, then neither can Job be fully aware of God's moral reasoning and actions.

It is the counsel of God spoken through the prophet Isaiah:

> For my [God's] thoughts are not your thoughts,
> neither are your ways my ways....
> As the heavens are higher than the earth,
> so are my ways higher than your ways
> and my thoughts than your thoughts. (Isaiah 55:8–9)

Still, Job was not reprimanded for questioning God. Braced like a man, he was willing to be authentic before God with his thoughts and even more willing to be authentic in his need to grow and in his desire to hear from God.

Job answered the Lord:

> I know that you can do all things;
> no plan of yours can be thwarted.
> You asked, "Who is this that obscures my counsel without
> knowledge?"
> Surely I spoke of things I did not understand,
> things too wonderful for me to know. (Job 42:2–3)

God tested Job. God corrected Job. God then restored Job, blessing him more than before. And Job was humbled. He even prayed on behalf of his friends who had spent hours trying to convince him that he must have committed some egregious sin in order for God to allow these things to come upon him.

An overworked phrase today is the one that begins with "Real men _____." According to God and Job, real men are honest and open before God, real men are not afraid to ask questions, real men admit when they are wrong, real men know when to shut up before God, and real men know that God is God and they are not.

The same holds true for real women.

KEEP YOUR EYES FIXED

Not long ago I was getting ready to speak at a conference when I was captivated by a rescue attempt being reported on television. Several children had been playing on a length of train track that spans a gorge when they heard a train coming. They began to sprint to get off the trestle and out of the way. They all made it to safety except one boy whose foot got stuck between the railroad ties.

The train was moving relatively slowly as it approached the bridge, but the engineer immediately knew the boy was in trouble. There was no way to stop the multiplied thousands of tons of metal that were bearing down on the frightened boy.

The young engineer had been instructed by some railroad veterans that if he ever found himself in such a predicament, he should avoid looking into the eyes of the person who was about to die. The older engineers told him he would be haunted by the memories, so to save himself from torment he should simply look away.

"But I just couldn't do that," the young engineer reported. "This was a kid."

Knowing time was short, the engineer worked his way to the front of the locomotive and balanced himself on the "pilot," what is popularly known as the "cowcatcher." He looked into the boy's eyes; the boy's eyes were fixed on him. The engineer had one shot and one shot only. With their eyes locked on each other, the burly man reached out and yanked the boy off the track, saving him from certain death.

It's a good thing the young engineer never took his eyes off the boy.

Who are you looking at to save you? What have you fixed your eyes upon?

Peter said, "Lord, if it's you, tell me to come to you on the water."

Jesus said, "Come."

Peter left the boat and "walked on the water and came toward Jesus. But when he saw the wind, he was afraid and, beginning to sink, cried out, 'Lord, save me!'" (Matthew 14:28–30).

Peter was so distracted by the wind that he took his eyes off Jesus. As he began to sink, he cried out to be saved. "Immediately Jesus reached out his hand and caught him" (Matthew 14:31).

The writer to the Hebrews reminds us: "Keep your eyes on *Jesus*, who both began and finished this race we're in. Study how he did it. Because he never lost sight of where he was headed—that exhilarating finish in and with God—he could put up with anything along the way: cross, shame, whatever. And now he's *there*, in the place of honor, right alongside God" (Hebrews 12:2, MSG).

And Paul said, "Brothers, I do not consider myself yet to have taken hold of it. But one thing I do: Forgetting what is behind and straining toward what is ahead, I press on toward the goal to win the prize for which God has called me heavenward in Christ Jesus" (Philippians 3:13).

Are your eyes fixed on Jesus, or are you too distracted by the problems around you? Are you running the race, living an authentic life before God and before the world, or are you tired, bogged down with worry, and quitting before the race gets fully under way? Are you straining forward toward the goal of winning the prize, or are you stuck in the mire of your past, attempting to hide from your friends, your family, yourself, and your God?

Authenticity requires that we keep our eyes on the only One who can save us. It requires that we realize that it was out of unending love that Jesus saved Peter when the disciple cried out. Jesus never reprimanded Peter for trying, only for taking his eyes off the Savior. It was that same love that caused God not to save Jesus when He cried out in the garden. Love led God to sacrifice His Son in order to save us.

Authenticity requires that we fight our battles in prayer and then experience the joy of graduation day. Authenticity requires that we press on to live out the greatest commandment, the one that says: "Love the Lord your God with all your heart and with all your soul and with all your mind and with all your strength" (Mark 12:30). And authenticity requires that we live out the second-greatest commandment: "Love your neighbor as yourself" (Mark 12:31).

God wants us to be real. He wants our eyes fixed firmly on Him. If we can't live authentically before God, neither will we be able to have an authentic relationship and be intimately involved in another person's life. Without authenticity before God, we will remain isolated and alone.

When we are completely real with God, we will know that the God-given answer to loneliness is love. God calls us to love Him. He calls us to love our neighbor.

And that truly is God's will.

Reflection

The Big Idea

To be truly authentic with other people, we must first be authentic with God. Being real with God means submitting to His will above our own while at the same time not being afraid to come before God with our true feelings and emotions. It means keeping our eyes fixed on Jesus while we honestly deal with all of the events of our day and of our heart. It also means accepting responsibility for our actions and failures. God's will is that we truly love Him and that we truly love our neighbor.

Key Verse

"'*Abba*, Father,' he said, 'everything is possible for you. Take this cup from me. Yet not what I will, but what you will.'" (Mark 14:36)

Answering Questions

- Are you afraid to come before God with your true feelings about the circumstances in your life? How authentic are you before God? Very? A little? Not at all? From what was discussed in this chapter, list ways you need to become more authentic before God.

- How are you at living in obedience to God's commands? Do you find yourself justifying your actions by saying God wants you to be happy, or do you consistently bring your life before God, allowing Him to examine your motives? Do you seek, on a daily basis, to be obedient to God? Prayerfully decide and write out how you are going to do things differently.

- Are you ready to change the world? Great, that's what God wants. But first, you must get real with Him.

Prayer

Sovereign and faithful God, it's easy for me to acknowledge Your complete control over the forces of the universe and the kingdom of heaven, yet all too often I fail to see Your power in my own life. Even more, I fail to fulfill Your desires for my life because I focus more on the things I think will make me happy than I do on following and obeying You. Lord, help me to seek You, as Jesus did, for the strength I need to do what You require of me. Help me to keep my eyes on You. Get it through my head, Lord, how vitally important it is for me to obediently love my neighbor. Amen.

Ten

Solving Loneliness

The Relational Gain of Letting God (and Others) Break In

You can accomplish anything in life,
provided that you do not mind who gets the credit.
—HARRY S. TRUMAN

Have you ever experienced a God interruption? I'll bet you have.

One of mine came many years ago while rock climbing without a belay line (a safety line to catch you if you fall). I was in a hurry, trying to get back to the top of the cliff where a dozen high school kids were waiting. I had just demonstrated the "safe" way to rappel down a cliff (*with* a belay line), and now I was violating my own instructions. I decided to save time by taking a short cut back to the top.

Having easily ascended about twenty-five feet to the first ledge, I now had another fifteen feet of rockface to scale that would bring me to a trail that would take me to the top. Yes, climbing fans, this was too high to be "bouldering." I was edging with my feet and had two fairly good crimpers—small holds for my fingers. At least that's what I thought.

Suddenly the edge that held my boot broke away; then one crimper gave way. I had only a few seconds, as I held on with three fingers, to try to guide my fall to a ledge ten feet below. If I missed the ledge, I'd plunge thirty-five feet to a hard landing on unforgiving rocks. When you're climbing—or I should say, when you're a climber who is falling—you're supposed to yell "falling." In this case, there was no one within earshot except God.

This is what I call a God interruption.

A God interruption is a moment or series of moments when an unplanned occurrence brings the few things that truly matter blazing to the front of your life. Such events don't put things in generic, human perspective; they put them in *God's* perspective. As I faced certain injury or even death if I missed the ledge below, God's precious gift of life and the innate desire for safety flooded my being. As I hung by three fingers with one foot slipping off a narrow ledge, I first wondered how I could have been so stupid as to try this. But that thought was quickly replaced by a series of images that passed almost in a blur:

- Life is precious, and I don't want to leave it just yet.
- Those high school kids need me. I'm here to love them and to talk to them about the love of God. Will my death push them away from God?
- Lord, I know it was my hurriedness that brought me here. Don't let my stupidity hurt my witness to these kids.
- I hope my folks will be okay.
- I've got to survive.

God interruptions bring to the surface what our heart knows to be true. All of our anger, hurriedness, denial, television escapism, and addictions come roaring to the forefront as God exposes our self-deception. If we listen to God when He barges into our out-of-whack world, we'll see that He is not seeking change just for the duration of the interruption. He's going for permanent changes that He wants in our hearts and in our lives.

Our Very Best Plans

Some of us put great stock in planning. We live by the adage that failing to plan is planning to fail. But I have another adage: if you want to make God laugh, show him your plans.

Several weeks ago I was planning to carve out some late-night hours to finish writing this book. I had a speaking engagement at a men's retreat looming, but otherwise I had nothing extra on the calendar.

Then there was a God interruption. It began on a Tuesday night.

Amy and I were walking through the gates of our school district's stadium to watch our oldest son, Austin, play football. He was to be the starting center that day, and he was pumped about it. My wife, ever the bargain hunter, saw that the booster club had school-spirit wear on sale and stopped to see if they had a sweatshirt for Austin. This caused her to miss the first couple of plays of the game. (We later realized God was protecting her.) As I was finding a seat in the bleachers, I saw a player being moved from the field. It was Austin, who soon was lying on the sideline in obvious pain.

As I mentioned in chapter 5, when I reached his side, it was easy to tell that this was no minor sprain. As a father of boys-who-are-all-boys, I knew more than the twenty-something sports trainer. So I looked him in the eye and said, "You need to quit working on my son now! We're taking him to the hospital."

An excruciatingly painful hour later we knew that our son had suffered a complete fracture through the growth plate of his femur as well as a dislocated knee. The surgery that followed didn't go as well as it could have. It was well past midnight as I sat in one of the most uncomfortable chairs God ever allowed to be manufactured, watching my son in a morphine-induced sleep.

This was a *major* God interruption.

All I cared about was my son's pain being taken away. All I could wonder was whether he would heal completely, if there would be any long-term effects, and what this injury might do to an energetic, fun-spirited, thirteen-year-old boy. Would he play football again, participate in tae kwon do (he's a black belt), or even be able to walk without pain when he's an adult? If there was only something I could do to spare my son all this pain.

Writing this book was important. Speaking at the coming men's retreat was important. Paying bills, keeping house, going to church—all those things were important. But a God interruption brings out the *best* things, the things that matter most, the things that matter to God.

Since that football game, my family's existence has been an exercise in letting other people know us and love us authentically. Friends took our other two children during that first night so Amy and I could stay at the hospital. Grandparents changed their plans so I could leave for a couple of days to speak at the men's retreat. The men understood my need to leave sooner than expected, to catch an earlier flight home, because Austin wasn't doing very well.

We've been loved.

Getting off the plane after seven hours of flying from the West Coast back to the Midwest, my cell phone was ringing. Amy was driving back to the hospital. Austin's fever had spiked, and there was a concern about infection. A friend had arranged for a different surgeon to meet with us. More friends were taking care of our other children.

This was a blurry twenty-one days. Caleb and Gracie were gracious, as they understood their parents needed extra time to be with Austin. Austin finally came home, and neighbors helped move my big-lug-of-a-son (remember, he's a lineman) when I had to be gone. People brought meals. We made countless hospital trips to have casts split, removed, and replaced. There were e-mails and phone calls and special arrangements to get the other two kids to and from school. I had to get to work. Teachers did extra work to make sure Austin kept up in his classes. Even the gal who cuts his hair offered to come by our house so he wouldn't have to maneuver his wheelchair and full-leg cast into her salon. I can't describe how badly Amy and I needed these acts of love and kindness.

I enjoy writing books. And it's great to speak at retreats. But compared to the life-giving experience of loving and being loved, knowing and being known, the events that normally occupy our time lose their urgency. After going through Austin's ordeal, deadlines didn't concern me as much. Other activities on the calendar just didn't seem as important as before. My son needed to get well, and to get well he needed his parents and a multitude of other people going the extra mile. In fact, Amy and I needed those other people desperately. We needed their love and care in a time of weakness and vulnerability.

God interruptions remind us that we need these things, and people.

BEING CHANGED AND CHANGING THE WORLD

God has placed in our hearts and souls a desire to change the world. As you and I come alive in Christ, we want to touch the hearts and souls of others. We want to be part of saving the world.

But how? If you're a person given to planning, you automatically grab a laptop and start working out a time line, with sequential action steps and a comprehensive strategy to guide the entire process. Planners plan. But in Scripture, we don't read a lot about detailed tactics. We don't even see much on innovative ways to share our faith, and we don't find a lot of model prayers for increasing our effectiveness. All of these are important things, certainly, but none of these is the most important thing.

Paul said, "And now these three remain: faith, hope and love. But the greatest of these is love" (1 Corinthians 13:13). It is love, not planning or better strategies or casting a vision, that changes the world. Paul's eyes were opened to what is most important: "If I…have not love, I am *nothing*" (1 Corinthians 13:2).

Musicians and poets know this is true. Most of the classic philosophers know it. Plato said, "At the touch of love, everyone becomes a poet."[1]

Dr. Martin Luther King Jr. said, "Without love, benevolence becomes egotism."[2]

John, the disciple Jesus loved, knew the bottom-line truth about love. "If anyone says, 'I love God,' yet hates his brother, he is a liar. For anyone who does not love his brother, whom he has seen, cannot love God, whom he has not seen" (1 John 4:20).

Jesus highlighted love in answering the rich man who wanted to get into the kingdom of God: "'Love the Lord your God with all your heart and with all your soul and with all your mind.' This is the first and greatest commandment. And the second is like it: 'Love your neighbor as yourself.' All the Law and the Prophets hang on these two commandments" (Matthew 22:37–40).

We have more than adequate precedent for pursuing love above all else, so what keeps us from doing it? What keeps us from loving God and changing the world through naked-soul relationships? Perhaps it's because we haven't truly taken time to reflect on what's going on inside us and what God is stirring in our souls.

Take a few moments right now to get quiet and reflect on the following. Ask God to open your eyes to the issues that most need your attention. Ask your loving Father to show you the most important things.

- It's okay that, deep inside, you really want to be liked. God made you that way, so stop worrying that you're just being needy. We're *all* needy in the sense that we need other people. It's how God made us. It's part of His strategy to free us from loneliness. You're not weak or overly needy. You're a person.

- Since you're a person, you need friends—the right kind of friends. No matter how independent you try to be, no matter how resourceful you are, friends are, as we say at my house, NAO—Not An Option. And this is an incredibly good thing, not a sign that you're somehow incomplete as a person.

- Since God created you, you have a very clear identity given to you by God. This, at a foundational level, answers the question, "Who am I?" You are a person loved by God and declared to be incredibly valuable. In fact, God places such high value on you that He sacrificed His Son just so He could have a relationship with you. That's how much you are loved.

- Do you preserve enough space in your life for God and for friends? Or do relationships get crowded out in your rush to get more stuff done? Do you need to deal with hurry sickness? Have you asked God to help you deal with it so relationships can thrive?

- Does your anger prevent you from deepening your relationships with other people? Have you asked those closest to you to give you honest feedback on how your anger affects them? Is God softening your heart and showing you ways to manage your anger?

- What about things in your life that substitute for authentic relationships? Are you settling for the cheap imitations, such as escaping into television shows or the temporary thrill of casual sex? Are you ready to accept the truth that recreational sex, or even the habit of following the lives of your favorite television personalities, do nothing but prolong your loneliness? Have you asked God to help you set television aside or to stop pursuing sex as a connection with others so you can start focusing on true, authentic relationships?

- Have you stopped growing? Have you settled for staying where you are? Has your heart become stagnant? Don't settle for a mediocre life. Begin following God, and see where He will lead you and who He will bring into your life. Tell Him you're willing to follow Him on this journey.

- Are you clinging to false security, settling for the "safety" of isolation to avoid the risk of authentic relationships? Are you afraid to be the person God created you to be and to allow others to get to know you as you really are? Have you asked God to give you the courage to risk transparency and vulnerability with others?

- Are you growing in the area of focusing on the needs of others rather than devoting your best efforts to addressing your own needs? Are you reorienting your life away from self and toward God and others? Have you asked God to give you the power to begin to overcome the universal human problem of selfishness?

- If you are married, are you truly naked, unashamed, and authentic before your spouse? Are you hiding anything? Are you likewise naked, unashamed, and authentic before your Maker? Or are you still trying to hide from Him, too?

- Have you wrestled with the essential but unsafe question, do I truly love God? And if you declared that, yes, you do love God, then does your life demonstrate that love through _____? You fill in the blank. Tell yourself what it means to love God.

SCALING THE STONY MOUNTAIN

I had a Greek language teacher in college who was more of a linguist than a Greek prof. We spent much more time discussing the origins of words than we did studying classic Greek, so I learned a lot of fascinating word trivia, just not much Greek. For instance, the English word *mediocre* comes from two Latin words, *medius,* meaning "the middle," and *ocres,* meaning a "rocky or stony mountain." Mediocre means to go halfway up, to the middle, of a rocky mountain—and then just stop.

I've had the thrill of climbing a couple of fourteeners in the Colorado Rockies—mountains that exceed fourteen thousand feet in elevation. In climbing such a peak, there are problems that nearly always arise—everything from freak storms to altitude sickness to blisters to a twisted ankle to dehydration or even a major injury. Still, every hiker I've met who sets out to ascend such a mountain has only one goal: to make it to the top. If they didn't reach the summit, it was usually due to something out of their control. A serious climber doesn't just sit down, take off her backpack, and say, "I think I'll just stop here. I know the view from the top far exceeds what I can see from here. Still, I can be satisfied with stopping just halfway up the mountain."

Mediocrity is beginning a project, a journey, or a relationship with the full intention of achieving excellence in the endeavor—but quitting when things get a little tough. People become satisfied with stopping halfway. And when they do, they cheat themselves out of the very best part of authentic relationships. They never make it to the top.

Pastor and author John Ortberg says that in almost everything we do, we reach a point where we are forced to choose which way to go.[3] One direction will put us on the path of least resistance—the easy way. This is the path that seems safe and secure. It allows us to hold on to hurts, to feel we've been unfairly used by others. It allows us to avoid the selflessness of offering forgiveness or confronting ourselves and others on matters that will deepen our relationships. The easy trail leads to mediocrity.

The other direction is much more difficult, requiring self-sacrifice. It leads to a life of meaning, joy, purpose, and authenticity. Ultimately, it brings us to the spectacular view from the top. But this trail is rocky and risky. There are steep inclines and narrow passages and cliffs that drop off to a deep canyon below. This route is not for the fainthearted. But it's the path that leads to freedom—the freedom that comes from breaking the chains of unforgiveness that bind us. It's the path that requires becoming real with those who have hurt us—and those whom we have hurt.

The easy path puts us with the majority of our peers, the people who are lonelier than we can imagine but who are willing to remain that way. They prefer the safety of isolation over the risk of authenticity. This path brings us to a life that no one wants. It's a life of aloneness in a passionless marriage or perhaps in a series of soul-draining romances. We get to a place where we realize that the easy path is actually the hardest place to live. It's "easy" only because it's superficial and halfhearted. It doesn't require anything of us. But in reality it's the harshest path because it leads to emptiness. It leaves us alone in life.

Then there's the steep path, which requires courage and determination. If you stay on that path and keep climbing, you'll find that loneliness is optional, not a given. This is the path that ends our loneliness by connecting us with others. It's the path that seeks God's desires over our own. It seeks to live by God's values, not the world's, so be aware that it will disrupt life as you have known it. It leads to changes in daily habits, assumptions, lifestyle. It might even lead to a job change, a career redirection, or other significant life alteration. No one said that pursuing authentic relationships means business as usual. It means just the opposite. The question is this: Where does God want you?

God wants us to climb the hard path. It requires much from us but ultimately brings ease and comfort to our soul. The rocky path involves allowing others to get inside your head and your heart, giving and receiving forgiveness, loving other people even when you don't feel loved, reaching out even when you feel neglected. The hard path is the *only* path that will deliver what your heart desires most, the depth of love you long for. The hard path leads to the end of loneliness and the connection and fulfillment that come through naked-soul relationships.

It has been said that many things in life—losing weight, financial management, following God—are *not* complicated, but they are difficult. It certainly applies here. The path to the top, the path to loving others, is not complicated. But, yes, it is difficult.

The Fork in the Road

When my primary career was counseling couples and individuals, I saw again and again the wreckage created by loneliness. And in almost every case, the damage could have been avoided if the person involved had chosen authenticity over hiding.

Mike had come to a fork in the road. He knew he had to do something about his double life. To most people who knew him, he was a successful youth leader in a parachurch ministry who also helped lead his church's singles group. He was the type of Christian man that single women loved to date. But they wouldn't have gone near him if they had known about his second life, a dark obsession with illicit sex. He regularly indulged in pornography, which led to compulsive masturbation.

Mike was dating Tonya, a woman who knew him as a personable and effective ministry leader. After dating for several months, he confessed to her that he had struggled with sexual temptation in the past. But he insisted that God had freed him from bondage. In some ways, his confession was true. It had been a long time since he had spent hours cruising the Internet looking for hard-core porn. But so-called soft-core pornography and habitual masturbation remained a regular part of his life.

Then came the fork in the road. Tonya used Mike's computer to check her e-mail and found the Web browser open to a page full of nude women. Shocked and sickened, she confronted Mike. "I thought you were done with all of this junk! So why are you looking at Internet pornography? Have you left it behind or not?"

Mike's first thought was to take the easy road. He could blame it on a friend who'd been using his computer. Or he could say that as he was researching another topic, that page just popped up, and that he then got interrupted by a phone call and forgot to close the page. Tonya was a trusting person, and he hoped she'd accept his excuse—even though it was a lie.

Then Mike looked into the eyes of the woman he really did want to know better. Finally he had found a woman he wanted to have a real relationship with, and she was asking him for the truth. He made the right decision, taking the hard road and telling Tonya everything.[4]

This is not a story where a guy is caught red-handed, decides to confesses, and his girlfriend immediately forgives him. And the power of her forgiveness makes it possible for the guy to never struggle again with illicit sex. That would be nothing more than a fairy tale.

In Mike's case, he saw the pain in the eyes of the woman he loved. He didn't want to lose her, and he knew that living a double life would mean the end of their relationship. He chose to take the path that led to being real with God and with people. Tonya needed time to think about his betrayal of her trust. And Mike knew he needed counseling and account-ability. The work of authenticity would include a lot of confession, a lot of prayer, a lot of soul searching, and submission to a few godly men who would keep him honest.

The hard road led to God's forgiveness and the beginning of true heal-ing from the hurts that had fueled Mike's double life.

TAKING A RISK

Professor and author Tony Campolo reports on a sociological study that included interviewing fifty people over the age of ninety-five. The senior citizens were asked, "If you had life to live over again, what would you do differently?" Through a variety of responses, three main ideas emerged.

If these people had another chance at life, they would

- risk more;
- reflect more;
- do more things that would last after they were gone.[5]

If they could return to their youth, they would go after their dreams, work to fulfill their personal missions, and take more chances in order to fulfill the desires of their hearts. In other words, they would take big risks.

Studies show that 92 percent of Americans say a successful marriage is important to them. Eighty-one percent of divorced Americans still believe that marriage should be a commitment to one person for a lifetime. And a vast majority of college students desperately want to have only one mar-riage in their life, and they want their marriage to be happy. But surveying the cultural landscape, they don't believe it's possible.[6] Other polls show that nearly two-thirds of children say they wish their parents had a job that gave them more free time so the family could do things together, while only 13 percent of children wish their parents made more money.[7] The

Bible says, "It is not good for people to be alone" (Genesis 2:18, author's paraphrase).

The late Kurt Cobain, head of the influential grunge band Nirvana, attempted suicide several times before he finally succeeded. In his pocket during an earlier suicide attempt was a note that referred to his parents' painful divorce, a situation known to have caused much of the hurt and despair in his life. The note simply read, "Nobody should have to go through the pain of a divorce."[8]

You were called to impact the world in which you live. You were called to bring joy, intimacy, and love. Staying and fighting for a marriage—not a physically abusive marriage, but one that has grown stale and unhappy—is risky. Giving up a professional track that you've worked hard to attain so you can be with your children more is risky. Sacrificing your own happiness for the good of others is risky. But by God's design, a good marriage, kids who feel important because they are worthy of your time, lonely people who now feel loved—all of these are achievable goals. And every one of them requires risk. Fifty people over the age of ninety-five understand that. They all would risk more.

THE IMPORTANCE OF REFLECTING

And those same people, if they could go back and do life again, would reflect more.

Throughout this book we have considered the importance of spending time alone reflecting on your life. In Scripture, the Creation narrative states: "By the seventh day God had finished the work he had been doing; so on the seventh day he rested from all his work" (Genesis 2:2). We also read that in God's economy, we are to "remember the Sabbath day by keeping it holy" (Exodus 20:8). But do you remember that God stopped and reflected throughout the days of Creation? As He created things to benefit His ultimate creation, women and men, He stopped, reflected, and "saw that it was good" (Genesis 1:10–25).

The beloved columnist Erma Bombeck wrote a book about children battling cancer. While reflecting on what these brave, hopeful children had taught her, she wrote:

> I had to look at them and question when I lost the child in me. When did I become so rigid that I couldn't shoot baskets with the kids because I had to clean out the refrigerator and change the baking soda?
>
> When did I look at a new puppy and see only puddles instead of something to love that would love me back?
>
> Was it the day I traded a live Christmas tree that filled the air with pungency for a practical "fake" tree that revolved, played a Christmas carol, and snowed on itself?
>
> And small things. How long it had been since I had looked at a piece of worthless broken glass and christened it a diamond because I had the power and the optimism to make something into anything I wanted it to be?
>
> The joys of eating snow and burnt marshmallows, burying myself in leaves, saving gum that had been chewed, throwing rocks, getting [my] feet wet, and kissing the dog had given way to greater expectations from life—none of which seemed to give the same joys as those had. Don't even think of asking me to close my eyes and hold out my hand for a surprise. Trust was one of the first things to go.
>
> When did I start dissecting relationships and all of their ramifications instead of simply asking, "You want to be my friend?"[9]

People who don't stop to reflect on the passing days neither appreciate the joys of simply living with others nor are they confronted with the realities of what they need to change, how they need to love, and who God is calling them to love. But major God interruptions do cause us to stop and reflect. In fact, we don't have to wait for God to interrupt. We can interrupt the constant flow of noise, information, and demands by stopping each day to reflect. Jesus said, "I tell you the truth, anyone who will not receive the kingdom of God like a little child will never enter it" (Mark 10:15). Part of receiving the kingdom of God is coming to God's world with a child's wide-eyed wonder. Adults have to purposely decide to view life through the eyes of a child. And for that to occur, we must take time for reflection.

THINGS THAT LAST LONGER THAN YOU

In the research involving people over the age of ninety-five, they said if they had a second chance they'd invest their lives in things that would remain after they were gone. The only investments we make during this life that count in eternity are time invested with God and time invested with people. What are you investing in? How many times have we heard people say that when they get just a little more time or money or accomplishments, *then* they'll hang out with their kids, go on vacation, spend time with their spouse, go on a mission trip, or get to know the neighbors? How many times have people said they can't wait until they retire so they can rest, relax, and enjoy life? Actress Elizabeth Hurley was quoted as saying, "We've got enough for our need but not enough for our greed.... I don't feel I can retire yet."[10] When we're only looking out for ourselves, how can there ever be enough? Our greed will change the world, but not in a way that any of us really wants.

And how many sermons have we heard on this parable:

The farm of a certain rich man produced a terrific crop. He
talked to himself: "What can I do? My barn isn't big enough for
this harvest." Then he said, "Here's what I'll do: I'll tear down
my barns and build bigger ones. Then I'll gather in all my grain
and goods, and I'll say to myself, 'Self, you've done well! You've
got it made and can now retire. Take it easy and have the time of
your life!'"

Just then God showed up and said, "Fool! Tonight you die.
And your barnful of goods—who gets it?"

That's what happens when you fill your barn with Self and
not with God. (Luke 12:16–21, MSG)

How many times do people reach the end of their life and say, "I just
wish I'd spent more time going to meetings, running errands, and cleaning
the house"?

Renowned preacher Dr. Haddon Robinson tells the following story:

Social worker Margaret Sangster told her colleagues about seeing
a young boy in an urban ghetto who appeared little more than a
bit of twisted human flesh. He had been struck by a car several
months earlier and had not received proper medical attention.

Although he was not a part of her caseload, she took the boy
to an orthopedist, who performed surgery on his legs. Two years
later the boy walked into Sangster's office without crutches. His
recovery was complete. Margaret recalled that as the two
embraced, she thought, *If I accomplish nothing else in my life, I
have made a real difference with at least this one!*

Sangster then told her colleagues, "This was all several years
ago now. Where do you think that boy is today?" They suggested

that he might be a teacher, a physician, or a social worker. With deep emotion, she responded, "No, he's in the penitentiary for one of the foulest crimes a human can commit." Then she said, "I was instrumental in teaching him how to walk again, but there was no one to teach him where to walk."[11]

Fifty people over the age of ninety-five said that if they had life to live over again, they would do more things that last into eternity. How many people are you teaching where to walk? As I ask you this question, I'm asking myself the same question.

MAKE IT ALL BETTER

Christian author and apologist Josh McDowell writes:

> The aloofness and distance that some adults might pass off as a youthful phase or temporary adolescent identity crisis are fast becoming a cultural condition. When our youths' sense of alienation and aloneness is not immediately and adequately addressed, and when they are left to themselves to find themselves, the distance they feel from adults becomes a relational isolation gap.
>
> Many members of this generation are isolated emotionally as well as relationally. They feel lost, not knowing who they really are.[12]

At the root of this pain for teenagers, adults, and kids alike is a sense of alienation and aloneness. What are we going to do about it?

Do you really want a life that matters? Do you want to make a difference in the world? Do you want to know the life-giving, naked-soul experience of knowing and being known, of loving and being loved? We achieve these things by taking the risk of reaching out, loving another human being, and letting that person get inside the heavily guarded walls of our heart. We must decide whether we are going to truly love or not. We have a choice. It's our move.

Years ago when I was living in an apartment, I was sitting out by the pool and reading. A child, no more than four, was playing in the water nearby. His was seeing how long he could let go of the side of the pool, flail his arms, then grab on again. It was an exciting game for him because the water was a couple of feet over his head.

I watched his game rather intently, mostly because his mother was distracted. She stood a few feet away, talking to a friend, with her back to the boy. After a few moments, the child's game ended when he sank to the bottom of the pool. I dropped my book, sprinted to the water, reached over the side of the pool, and pulled out a rather surprised and scared little boy.

I'm not sure why, but God has given me numerous opportunities to save children from serious injury. There was a time when a group of us were standing around the bleachers after a baseball game. One of the player's sons came walking toward us—right off the top row. I caught him before he hit the ground. Another time I was at a church function when I saw some younger kids bouncing on a trampoline. I was twenty feet away but sensed I needed to walk over. I arrived just in time to catch a five-year-old flying through the air. I guess I know why I've been there to help these kids at crucial moments. It's because I was watching and anticipating their need.

We can't stop all human suffering, but we can prevent a lot of pain if we just watch for ways to help. We can eliminate the suffering caused by loneliness if we just open our eyes and look at the neighbors God wants us to love.

The world is full of people who are dying from loneliness, and, ironically, the sea they are drowning in is a sea of people. We need to watch and anticipate that the kid in the pool may be going under. We need to watch and anticipate that the people who live next door and who seem so busy may also be very lonely people. They might have everything they want except for the thing they want most: a friend.

Are you willing to leave the comfort and safety of your home to change the world? Are you willing to deal with the "stuff" that keeps you from living a life that matters? Are you ready to let go of your security and deal with your fear of risk, openness, and vulnerability?

Fear keeps us from loving our neighbors as we have been called to do. We will be scared to deal with all the barriers—the pace of life, noise, addictions, television, anger, selfishness, a neighbor's initial wariness—because we don't want to be vulnerable. We'll be scared to say, "Will you be my friend," because we're too grown up for that. We'll be scared to be a neighbor like the good Samaritan because we don't want to have our hearts broken. We're scared, but we have to get over it.

C. S. Lewis said it best:

> There is no safe investment. To love at all is to be vulnerable. Love anything, and your heart will certainly be wrung and possibly broken. If you want to make sure of keeping it intact, you must give your heart to no one, not even an animal. Wrap it carefully round with little hobbies and little luxuries; avoid all entanglements; lock it up safe in the casket or coffin of selfishness. But in that casket—safe, dark, motionless, airless—it will

change. It will not be broken; it will become unbreakable, impenetrable, irredeemable. The alternative to tragedy, or at least to the risk of tragedy, is damnation. The only place outside Heaven where you can be perfectly safe from all the dangers and perturbations of love is Hell.[13]

To climb the steep trail and live in authentic relationships, we will seek to make others feel safe, at risk to our own hearts. We will choose not to belittle, but instead to care and confront. We will decide to support others in any way we can, even when being there is hard.

We can love. We can risk. We can live a life that matters. And in doing so, we'll change the world.

We can start by loving our neighbor, including those who live in our home. We will let them love us as well. And we will allow them to know us, fully and intimately.

It is not complicated—"Love your neighbor"—but it is difficult.

I hope and pray that we dance with others—in intimacy and individuality—for the rest of our lives.

Reflection

The Big Idea

God is the author and creator of the greatest thing in the world: love. Real love can change our life. It can change the lives of our neighbors. It can cause us to risk more, reflect more, and do more things that will last after we leave this earth. It is love that led Jesus to the cross, and love that raised Him from the dead. It is love that can change the world—even your little corner of it.

Key Verses

"If anyone says, 'I love God,' yet hates his brother, he is a liar. For anyone who does not love his brother, whom he has seen, cannot love God, whom he has not seen. And he has given us this command: Whoever loves God must also love his brother." (1 John 4:20–21)

"And now these three remain: faith, hope and love. But the greatest of these is love." (1 Corinthians 13:13)

Answering Questions

- Have you had any "God interruptions" in your life? Even without them, have you taken the time to discover and reflect on what is truly important in your life? Make a list.
- Are you ready to fight against the pushes and pulls of this culture and live your life for what is truly important, both for you and for God? Are you ready to begin watching "with the eyes of God," looking for ways to love and serve others on a daily basis? Write down how you are going to do that.
- Are you ready to change the world? Are you serious about it? Then go back through all the questions and everything you underlined or highlighted. Get an accountability partner and start praying and start walking. You will be amazed at what love will do.

Prayer

Lord God, You are the creator of loneliness, and You are the creator of the answer to the loneliness problem, because you are the author and creator of love. Help me to be a better lover. Show me, every day, the power of love to change my own life and the lives of others. Fill me with a love and compassion for the world that is so full that it can't help but overflow into the lives of lonely and hurting people.

May I love You, Father, more and more each day, and may that love be demonstrated by my daily love of my neighbor. It is there that the world will start to become what You desire it to be. Bless me, Lord, so that I may serve and bless others.

In the name of the One who taught me what love truly is, Jesus Christ. Amen.

Does It Matter on Monday?

When I was on the teaching and preaching staff of a large Midwestern church, we often asked ourselves if what we taught and preached on Sunday really mattered on Monday. Did our words help people live more God-honoring lives? Did our counsel and our teaching comfort people in their hurts? Did everything we said encourage people to follow Christ more faithfully?

Did it matter on Monday?

At the beginning of this book, I stated that nothing matters more to us than that we matter to someone. Now it's Monday—do you matter to someone? Does someone matter to you in honest and authentic ways?

At the beginning of this book, I also asked a series of questions:

- Do you want to live a life that matters?
- Do you want to change the world?
- Do you want to be loved?
- How, in the middle of the most technologically connected, people-surrounded culture in history, are we also surrounded by so many incredibly lonely people?

Now that we're about to end this book, what are your answers?

I've said again and again that the road to naked-soul relationships is never easy, and it is seldom safe. Finding the end of your loneliness always requires taking big risks. God knew what He was doing when He told us the two most important things in the world are to love God with everything we are and then to authentically love our neighbors in a way that changes them, changes us, and changes the world.

You're lonely, and so is your neighbor. It's Monday. What are you going to do?

TRAPPED IN A "CUBE"

It has been said that anonymity is the enemy of civility. In other words, the less we authentically know people, the easier it is to be rude, mean, and even downright cruel. It's why there is so much road rage and why we send an e-mail to someone who is sitting five feet away rather than going over to talk to the person.

I recently was talking with a man who most of his life has lived in various parts of Europe and Africa. One of the things that troubles him about the Western work environment is that so many people work in "cube land." We are gathered in a relatively small area, but we're separated from one another by office cubicles. That was new to this man. Western business experts think it's efficient. The cartoon strip *Dilbert* satirizes it. My friend thinks it breeds distrust and a lack of personal interaction.

As I thought about office cubes, I realized they are highly efficient and also incredibly effective in minimizing and even devaluing relationships. Just like e-mail, cell phones, instant messaging, Internet chat rooms, workers who telecommute, television, and pagers. They all breed anonymity and isolation, producing more time spent alone and less time engaging directly with other people. They give rise to more self-concern and self-absorption and less kindness shown toward others. All of this feeds our loneliness.

The cure for self-absorption is loving others. The cure for pervasive anonymity is loving others. The cure for unkindness is loving others. The cure for loneliness—yours and your neighbor's—is loving others.

It's Monday. What are you going to do?

THE GREATEST THING

Our church recently hosted a worship team from our sister church in Nairobi, Kenya. As our visitors led us through times of song and prayer, the worship leader asked everyone to greet those around them and get to know one another better. "This is church," she said. "No one should be alone here."

She's right. No one *should* be alone, but there are many in our churches, our neighborhoods, our places of business, and even in our homes who are achingly alone. The question is, what type of God interruption is it going to take for you to reach out to end their loneliness?

Shortly after the tragic events of September 11, 2001, country singer and songwriter Alan Jackson got up late one night and wrote down the words to the song "Where Were You When the World Stopped Turning?" The soulful song is the epitome of what God interruptions can cause. At the end of the chorus, Jackson sings: "Faith, hope, and love are some good things he [God] gave us. And the greatest is love."[1]

The lyric echoes Paul's words from 1 Corinthians 13. Love is the greatest virtue because it heals us and gives us hope. Love was the ultimate demonstration of faith when it went to the cross. As a licensed mental health counselor, I may get in trouble for saying this, but it seems to me that people today are far too quick to run to counselors with issues and problems when what they really need is an experience of authentic love from a neighbor. Therapy certainly has its place and purpose, but I can't help but wonder what would happen if we all believed in and lived out on a daily basis the phenomenal power of God's creation of love.

Scripture tells us that we love others because God loved us first (1 John 4:19). Just as God's love gives us strength and acceptance and a place to belong, our love toward others does a similar work in their lives. John goes on to tell us: "Whoever loves God must also love his brother" (1 John 4:21).

In other words, loving others is not optional.

You might recall the old story about a boy who wanted a dog. Each day the boy's journey home from school took him by the local animal shelter; no matter the weather, he would always stop and watch as the puppies played out in their fenced yard. One day he saw the puppy he wanted. He was so thrilled. He ran, as best he could, all the way home to tell his parents. "Mom, Dad," he cried, "I found a puppy I want to buy; he's great."

They, too, were excited and told him he could get the puppy as soon as he saved enough money for the adoption fee. Fully determined, the boy worked hard, he saved every penny, and he even skimped on lunch to save some extra change. His parents even added a little to his bank account when he wasn't looking. Then the day finally arrived that he had enough money.

He loaded up his pockets, walked proudly down the street to the shelter, marched confidently up to the manager, put his money on the counter, and said to the man behind it, "Mister, I want to adopt a puppy."

"That's great, young man," the manager said. "Which one?"

The boy proudly pointed to the yard. "I want that one," he said, grinning, "that black and white spotted one over in the corner."

Without even realizing it, the manager's smile quickly turned to a frown. "Oh, son," he said, "you don't want *that* puppy. Pick a different one; I know you'll be a lot happier."

"No," the little boy kindly replied, "that's the one I want. Here's my money. Will you get him for me please?"

"Son," the man came back, "I'm telling you, you don't want *that* puppy. He's not like the other ones. He won't be able to run and play with you like another dog could. Now, trust me, I know best. Pick another puppy. You'll be much happier."

Sternly but still politely the boy replied, "No sir, I know about that puppy. I've been watching him every day. I know everything about him. And I've been saving my money just for him. *That* is the puppy I want."

Frustrated the manager finally said, "Now, son, I don't know any other way to tell you this but the reason you don't want that puppy is because he is crippled. I told you he can't play with you like the other dogs can. As a matter of fact, that puppy is going to be put to sleep in a few days. Now, pick another puppy; you will be much, much happier."

The little boy, with his eyes starting to mist over, slowly stepped backward from the counter. He reached down with both hands and pulled up the legs of his pants. As he did, he revealed metal braces running up both sides of both legs. While holding his pants high, he looked into the manager's eyes and said, "Mister, you just don't understand what love can do."

God picks us, not caring that we're weak and broken or that we've been shoved off to the side. In fact, He seems to love us more because of the things we're least proud of. His love strengthens us in the weak places.

God's love is the only workable strategy for changing the world. He knows full well what love can do.

It's Monday. Do *you* know what love can do?

It's Time to Change the World

The Bible says, "The command we have from Christ is blunt: Loving God includes loving people. You've got to love both" (1 John 4:21, MSG). The cure for your own loneliness is to reach out to others. They are as lonely as you are. The only cure is love.

God calls us to trust Him more than we do ourselves and to take the risk of exposing our soul. Naked-soul love is God's amazing, everyday solution to your loneliness and mine.

Prayerfully wrestle with these four challenges, then choose one that you will do this week. Next week try another one. And never stop.

1. God is looking for people to change the world through love. Will it be you? If so, list five people who need to be loved authentically. Now go love them.

2. Are you the one who is lonely? Have you been hoping and praying that someone will reach out to you? Do you understand that you have to make the first move, that you must reach outside yourself and touch another person's life? Will you do that? Realize that you already know five other people who are just as lonely as you are. List their names, then reach out to them. Talk to them, face to face, without hiding or pretending to be someone you're not. Take a risk that they might not respond the way you'd like them to. Love them anyway.

3. Do you understand the power that sent Jesus to the cross and then brought him back from the grave? Find a quiet place and spend five minutes a day—just five minutes—meditating and thinking about the love that sacrificed so much and then brought such hope to each of us. Over and over, let your mind and heart fill with the idea, "God loves *me* that much!"

4. Do you want to live a life that matters? Then pray that God will make your heart overflow with His love. Pray that you will grow every day

in your understanding of the power of His love. Then ask God to open the door for you to find ways to come out of hiding, to take the big risks, to reach out to others, and to begin to put into practice God's amazing, everyday answer to loneliness. Risk loving someone else, not holding anything back. If you encounter pain or rejection, know that Jesus did too. Now risk some more. Love someone again.

It's Monday, and the lonely world is waiting.

Notes

Foreword

1. Richard E. Byrd, *Alone: The Classic Polar Adventure* (New York: Adventure Library, 2003).

Prologue: Find a Life That Matters

1. Larry Viskochil, "Teaching History with Photographs," *Illinois History Teacher* 5, no. 2 (1998): 46.

2. "Major Depression Facts," Depression Learning Path, Uncommon Knowledge, http://www.clinical-depression.co.uk/Depression_Information/facts.htm.

3. "People (Who Need People)," lyrics by Bob Merrill; music by Jule Styne. Published by Chappell and Co., Inc., Los Angeles, Calif., 1964.

Chapter 1: God Created Loneliness, Then He Solved It

1. "Only the Lonely," music and lyrics by Roy Orbison and Joe Melson. Published by Monument Records, Hendersonville, Tenn., 1960.

2. "Eleanor Rigby," music and lyrics by John Lennon and Paul McCartney. Published by Song/ATV Tunes, Nashville, 1966.

3. "Baby One More Time," performed by Bowling for Soup. Music and lyrics by Martin Sandberg. Published by Zomba Enterprises, Inc., Beverly Hills, Calif., 2003.

4. "All Is Loneliness," music and lyrics by Janis Joplin. Published by Sony Music, Nashville, 1972.

5. *The Truth About Cats and Dogs,* Audrey Wells, prod. Cari-Esta Albert, dir. Michael Lehmann (Beverly Hills: Twentieth Century Fox, 1996).

6. Stephen Lazarus, "Hardwired to Connect," *Capital Commentary* (January 26, 2004): 1.

7. From monologue of *Late Night with Conan O'Brien.* Starring Conan O'Brien, produced by Lorne Michaels, directed by Allan Kartun, 2003.

Chapter 2: Alone or Just Lonely?

1. James Lynch, *A Cry Unheard: New Insights into the Medical Consequences of Loneliness* (Baltimore: Bancroft, 2000), 79.

2. Linda Waite and Maggie Gallagher, *The Case for Marriage* (New York: Doubleday, 2000), 47–64.

3. Lynch, *A Cry Unheard,* 213.

4. Lynch, *A Cry Unheard,* 214.

5. Sigmund Freud, "On Narcissism: An Introduction," in *The Standard Edition of the Complete Psychological Works of Sigmund Freud* (London: Hogarth Press, 1957), 24:100.

6. Patrick Mullahy, *Psychoanalysis and Interpersonal Psychiatry: The Contributions of Harry Stack Sullivan* (New York: Science House, 1970), 253.

7. Les Parrott and Leslie Parrott, *Relationships* (Grand Rapids: Zondervan, 1998), 19–39.

8. Parrott and Parrott, *Relationships,* 21.

9. C. S. Lewis, *The Four Loves,* audio recording (Waco, TX: Word, 1994).

Chapter 3: Who Are You, Really?

1. Fred Rogers, (commencement address, Marquette University, Milwaukee, WI, 2001), http://www.marquette.edu/commencement/2001/address.html.

2. Market Trends Report, "Oprah: A Heavenly Body?" *U.S. News & World Report,* March 31, 1997, 18.

3. Frans de Waal, *The Ape and the Sushi Master: Cultural Reflections of a Primatologist* (New York: Basic Books, 2001), 46.

4. David Riesman, *Faces in the Crowd: Individual Studies in Character and Politics* (North Stratford, NH: Ayer, 1979).

5. "How Much Does It Cost?" was used with the permission of its author.

Chapter 4: Do You Love God?

1. *Webster's Revised Unabridged Dictionary*, s.v. "hate," http://www .dictionary.com.

2. Max Lucado, *The Applause of Heaven* (Dallas: Word, 1990), chapter 18.

3. To read Jesus's version of this parable, see Luke 10:29–37.

4. Closely related to the question, who is my neighbor? is the question, who is my brother? While a neighbor is anyone in need, a brother is any person within the household of faith. Paul delivered a scathing indictment against those who treat fellow believers with disdain, hatefulness, and vengeance (see 1 Corinthians 6:5–8). On the contrary, Paul taught that we should give fellow believers preferential treatment as we engage in doing good for others (see Galatians 6:10). That is, if we love God.

5. Barna Research Group, Ltd., *Twentysomethings Struggle to Find Their Place in Christian Churches* (Ventura, CA: Barna Research Group, 2003). See www.barna.org.

6. John Grisham, *The Street Lawyer* (New York: Doubleday, 1999), 15–16, emphasis added.

Chapter 5: Losing Friends in the Red Zone

1. *Life*, February 21, 1964, 91–93.

2. Many of my thoughts on the disease of hurry were inspired by the speaking and writing of John Ortberg, teaching pastor at Menlo Park Presbyterian Church in California. As I have studied and taught on this subject and counseled countless people caught in this struggle, it is

sometimes difficult to recall the source of every idea. I deeply appreciate John's good thinking on this crucial topic.

3. John Ortberg, "Diagnosing Hurry Sickness," *Leadership Journal* 19, no. 4 (fall 1998): 31.

4. Robert Levine, *A Geography of Time: The Temporal Misadventures of a Social Psychologist, or How Every Culture Keeps Time Just a Little Bit Differently* (New York: Basic Books, 1998), 151.

5. "Hospital Has Express Lane," *USA Today*, July 17, 1991, 01-A.

6. Bill Hybels, "A Faith That Works: Destructive Desires," audiotape (Barrington, IL: Seeds Tape Ministry, Willow Creek Community Church, 1998).

7. Lewis Grant, quoted in John Ortberg, *The Life You've Always Wanted* (Grand Rapids: Zondervan, 1997), 87–88.

8. Charles E. Hummel, *Tyranny of the Urgent!* (Downers Grove, IL: InterVarsity, 1967), 4.

9. Brother Lawrence, *The Practice of the Presence of God: With Spiritual Maxims* (Old Tappan, NJ: Fleming Revell, 1999).

10. Brother Lawrence, quoted in John Ortberg, "Taking Care of Busyness," *Leadership Journal* 19, no. 4 (fall 1998), http://www.ctlibrary .com/le/1998/fall/814028.html.

Chapter 6: Unplug the Microwave Life

1. Socrates, quoted in William McRae, "Making of a Christian Marriage" (sermon, Believer's Chapel, Dallas, 2000), http://www.believers-chapel.org/resources/christianmarriage.htm.

2. Newton Hightower, *Anger Busting 101* (Houston: Bayou Publishing, 2002), 25.

3. *Moody Monthly,* December 1989, 72.

4. From *Archie Bunker's Place*, CBS television, Joe Gannon, prod. Mort Lachman. Aired from 1979 to 1983.

5. Dr. Vernon Grounds, president emeritus, Denver Theological Seminary (sermon, 1982).

6. Dan McKean, "Merchants of Death," *Faith Today*, January 20, 2002, http://www.faithmag.com/todaysfaith/2002/1-20-02.html.

Chapter 7: Sex and the Idiot Box

1. Tim Alan Gardner, *Sacred Sex* (Colorado Springs, CO: WaterBrook, 2002), 162–63.

2. Gardner, *Sacred Sex*.

3. Edward T. Welch, *Addictions: A Banquet in the Grave* (Phillipsburg, NJ: P&R Publishing., 2001), xvi.

4. Testimony cited in the Senate Committee on the Judiciary, *Children, Violence, and the Media*, September 14, 1999.

5. Senate Committee on the Judiciary, *Children, Violence, and the Media*.

6. John Ortberg, *The Life You've Always Wanted* (Grand Rapids: Zondervan, 1997), 76.

7. "Study of Entertainment Media," Henry J. Kaiser Family Foundation, http://www.kff.org.

8. "Facts and Figures About Our TV Habit," http://www.tvturnoff.org/images/facts&figs/factsheets/FactsFigs.pdf.

9. Teenage Life Online: "The Rise of the Instant-Message Generation and the Internet's Impact on Friendships and Family Relationships," The Pew Internet and American Life Project, www.pewinternet.org (accessed June 20, 2001).

10. Haddon Robinson, "The Disciple's Prayer" (sermon, Denver Seminary Chapel, 1982).

11. Attributed to C. S. Lewis in *Shadowlands,* HBO Studios. Directed by Richard Attenborough. 1993.

12. Dallas Willard, *Hearing God* (Downers Grove, IL: InterVarsity, 1999), 155.

Chapter 8: Selfishness, Security, and Stagnation

1. Martin Kasindorf, "Schwarzenegger Calls Bush an 'Ally' of Calif.," *USA Today,* October 16, 2003, http://www.usatoday.com.

Chapter 9: Getting Real with God

1. "God Is God," music and lyrics by Steven Curtis Chapman (Brentwood, TN: Sparrow Records, 2001).

Chapter 10: Solving Loneliness

1. Plato, quoted in "Love Poems and Quotes," The Board of Wisdom, www.boardofwisdom.com.

2. Martin Luther King Jr., quoted in Best Inspirational Quotes, http://www.bestinspirationalquotes.com/success-leaders/dr-martin-luther-king.htm.

3. John Ortberg, "Facing the Fork in the Road" (sermon, Willow Creek Community Church, Barrington, IL, 1998).

4. This story is a composite picture of several counseling clients who came to me for help. The details of the story provide an accurate depiction of the damage that is done by loneliness.

5. Tony Campolo, *Who Switched the Price Tags?* (Waco, TX: Word, 1986), 28–29.

6. Sources of statistics are as follows: 92% say marriage is important: Linda Waite and Maggie Gallagher, *The Case for Marriage* (New York: Double-

day, 2000), 142; 81% of divorced: Waite and Gallagher, *The Case for Marriage*, 37; the aspirations and hopes of college students: Arthur Levine and Jeanette S. Cureton, *When Hope and Fear Collide: A Portrait of Today's College Student* (San Francisco: Jossey-Bass, 1998), 95.

7. Betsy Taylor, *What Kids Really Want That Money Can't Buy* (New York: Warner Books, 2003). Found at The Center for a New American Dream, http://www.newdream.org.

8. Kurt Cobain, quoted in Charles Colson, *How Now Shall We Live?* (Carol Stream, IL: Tyndale, 1999), 139, 324.

9. Erma Bombeck, *I Want to Grow Hair, I Want to Grow Up, I Want to Go to Boise: Children Surviving Cancer* (New York: Harper & Row, 1989), 140–41.

10. "Out Loud," *US Weekly*, November 11, 2002, 36.

11. Haddon W. Robinson, "Wholeness of Life," *Our Daily Bread*, October 26, 1998, www.gospelcom.net/rbc/odb-10-26-98.shtml.

12. Josh McDowell, *The Disconnected Generation* (Nashville: Word, 2000), 19.

13. C. S. Lewis, *The Four Loves* (Ft. Washington, PA: Harvest Books, 1971), 121.

Epilogue: Does It Matter on Monday?

1. "Where Were You When the World Stopped Turning?" music and lyrics by Alan Jackson (Nashville: Arista Records, 2001).

If you would like to contact Tim Gardner,
please write to him at one of the following addresses:

Tim@timgardner.org

http://www.timgardner.org

Dr. Tim Gardner
The Marriage Institute
P.O. Box 602
Westfield, IN 46074

To learn more about WaterBrook Press and view
our catalog of products, log on to our Web site:
www.waterbrookpress.com

WATERBROOK
PRESS